Japanese Lacquer

FROM
SOUTHERN CALIFORNIA
COLLECTIONS

PACIFIC ASIA MUSEUM

PASADENA · 1991

Copyright ©1991, Pacific Asia Museum
ISBN 1-877921-06-8

Photographs by Raymond Atchley and William Hawkes
Printed by The Castle Press
Pasadena, California

JAPANESE LACQUER

FROM SOUTHERN CALIFORNIA COLLECTIONS

Cover:
Suzuribako (writing box)
Meiji Period

Design of net of fireflies with some escaping. A reference to the story of the "poor scholar," next to a panel of textured wood with silver and gold lacquered grasses, inlaid with shell and the crescent moon.
Inside cover has *togidashi* design of egrets on a willow by a stream. *Nashiji* ground. Interior with inkstone, ink stick, brush, and knife, and bronze *suiteki* in the form of a water pot.
From the collection of Bob and Elly Nordskog

CONTENTS

Foreword vii

Introduction 1

Catalogue 5

Glossary 29

Bibliography 33

Acknowledgments 35

FOREWORD

SOUTHERN CALIFORNIA has been the home to collectors of Oriental art of all kinds, but is particularly rich in the beautiful art form known as Japanese art lacquers.

Several distinguished collections of these superb objects are to be found in the Los Angeles area and we are extremely pleased to be able to present outstanding examples from several of these important collections.

This is in no way intended to be a survey of Japanese lacquer, or even a complete picture of the holdings of these objects to be found in Southern California. What we have done is select objects of particular beauty, many of which have not been exhibited before, to share with the public.

Virginia Atchley has written in this publication a most illuminating essay on lacquer, with an explanation of one form of lacquer art—the *inro*—since our exhibition contains more examples of *inro* than any other type of lacquer. She has also provided an extensive glossary and bibliography.

I would like to thank Virginia for the characteristically generous manner in which she has shared her knowledge about lacquer, and also for loaning us many superb examples from her collection. I would also like to thank Elly Nordskog who has loaned many exquisite lacquers from her collection and has also been most generous with her time and knowledge.

I would also like to thank Joe and Etsuko Price for sharing some important lacquer objects from their renowned collection. Other collectors who have been more than generous by allowing us to borrow objects from their collection include Mr. Robert L. Chasin, Mr. John Crowley, Mrs. Emma Dagan, Mr. and Mrs. Henry Foster, Mrs. Ann Meselson, Dr. and Mrs. William Mizener, Mrs. Margaret M. Palmer, and several anonymous donors.

Japanese lacquer has sometimes been considered by Western scholars to be a craft rather than a fine art. I hope that this exhibition will help dispel that misconception, as it will be obvious to the most inexperienced visitor that these objects are, indeed, superb works of art, worthy of our admiration and attention.

DAVID L. KAMANSKY
Director,
Pacific Asia Museum

INTRODUCTION

JAPANESE LACQUER is one of the most highly developed art forms the world has known. One can well appreciate, on viewing the pieces shown in this exhibition, Louis Gonse's[1] enthusiastic statement made a hundred years ago, that "Japanese lacquered objects are the most perfect works that have issued from man's hands."

Lacquered objects appeared in Japan in prehistoric times, but it was not until the sixth or seventh centuries, after the introduction of Buddhism in Japan, that her lacquer art history really began. At first she copied from the Chinese but soon her artists began to evolve their own styles and designs; as early as the Nara period (eighth century) lacquer appeared that was quite different from Chinese lacquer. For some time the greatest demand for lacquer was for use in the shrines and temples, and by the nobility, but gradually lacquered objects of many kinds were made, and the growing number of lacquer artists applied their talents to boxes of various types and sizes, as well as on furniture, sword scabbards, and other secular objects.

Most interestingly, and importantly, they continually invented new techniques which they proceeded to develop to a peak of perfection and variety that has never been rivaled. Some techniques, especially with carved lacquer, were borrowed from the Chinese, but the majority they originated themselves. The most important Japanese invention was called *makie*.

The word *makie* made its first appearance in print in the ninth century. Literally it means "sprinkled picture"—and it is a process that involves drawing a design in lacquer on a carefully prepared ground and then, before the lacquer dries, sprinkling it with gold or silver dust, sometimes colored powders. The point is that the design is not, as always before, painted on with a brush, using powders bound together with glue, but is sprinkled onto the still damp drawing. When this layer is dried and polished, the process is repeated many times. In other words, the *makie* technique consists essentially of building up the design by repeated applications of lacquer followed by metallic dustings and rubbings. By thus applying lacquer to specific areas of the design rather than to the entire surface, the artist can obtain varying degrees of relief and delicate shadings, and the individual specks of gold, brought out by the repeated polishings, glisten. At the same time a lovely lustrous finish is created and a sense of depth, even when the final surface is completely flat. It might be pointed out that the *makie* technique allows no margin for error because there is no way to remove the dustings from the sticky lacquered surface.

The most important types of *makie*, given in the order of their historical development, are three: *togidashi, hiramakie,* and *takamakie.*

---
1. Gonse, L. *L'Art Japonais,* Paris, 1883.

In *togidashi,* which literally means to "bring out by rubbing," the finished design is completely covered with several layers of lacquer, usually black, which are then very carefully polished down with charcoal until the top layers are worn away and the sprinkled design reappears. As a result of this gradual grinding down, the design is now on exactly the same plane as the surrounding ground. Then the whole surface is coated with transparent lacquer, which, in turn, is polished. The finished effect is an absolutely even, flat, softly shimmering surface. One special type of *togidashi,* known as *sumie,* produced a very distinctive effect. Powdered charcoal sprinkled into a silver (sometimes gold) ground and then rubbed down resulted in a design that closely resembled an ink painting (*sumie*).

Hira means "flat" so *hiramakie* is a "flat sprinkled picture." It is easier to make than *togidashi:* the sprinkled design is simply covered with transparent lacquer and polished to a fine gloss. Because the design is not polished down, as in *togidashi, hiramakie* is, in fact, not strictly flat but slightly raised from the surface. *Taka* means "raised," so *takamakie* is a "raised sprinkled picture," wherein the decoration is first applied in relief and then sprinkled so that varying heights can be achieved. *Takamakie,* which originated in the fourteenth century and was fully developed in the fifteenth, is perhaps the most distinctive feature of Japanese lacquer and surely the one requiring the most patience.

The three basic types of *makie* are often combined in numerous ways. They are also combined with inlay and incrustation work of many kinds of materials: mother-of-pearl, awabi and other shell, ivory, metal, faience, porcelain, pottery, hardstones and the like. Moreover, there are more than four hundred refinements of the *makie* technique, depending upon the type and fineness of the metal powders, the over-lacquerings and polishings, no polishing, and so on—each with its own distinctive name.

Makie lacquer is unique to Japan and over the years was brought to an artistic and technical perfection which no country, including China (who tried), has ever been able to imitate successfully.

The Japanese lacquerers worked in family workshops, carrying on from son to son (or adopted son), for sometimes as many as twenty generations. There were many renowned family dynasties, running anywhere from the fifteenth century through the nineteenth, such as the Koma, Koami, Kajikawa, Yamada (Jokasai), Shunsho, and Tatsuke. However, there is great confusion and uncertainty in most attempts to distinguish among the artists in any one family group and indeed sometimes between the schools themselves (such as the Kajikawa and the Yamada, for example). It should be remembered that signatures in Japanese art, except on painting, were not important. In lacquer they were rarely used at all until the eighteenth century and then only on small objects, such as inro. Yet some of the finest inro are unsigned, and we know that many of the best artists worked for the daimyos and the imperial and shogunate courts where an artist's signature on his work would have been an arrogant breach of decorum.

In short, we have surprisingly little information about lacquer artists, and a definite lineage, in fact, of only one family, the Koma. The student and collector therefore must rely, in many instances, upon a comparison of styles and techniques to come up with even a tentative attribution of date and specific artist. As Casal[2] says, "Even with much experience, it is therefore practically impossible to be categorical about an object's date." However, an English scholar, E. A. Wrangham, has been at work for years on a comprehensive and detailed comparative study of lacquer artists, their styles, techniques, and signatures, in the hope of providing reasonably accurate datings and identifications of artists throughout—a daunting task which may soon be ready for publication.

Of all the forms that Japanese art lacquer takes, that of the inro is the best known to Westerners and the one most assiduously collected. There are probably several reasons for this, the first being its small compact size requiring little space for keeping and displaying. The various lacquer boxes, of which the writing box (*suzuribako*) is the most popular, are too large for many collectors, and many suffered damage through the years. Then too the inro is a unique invention of the Japanese; there is nothing anywhere else in the world like it. Still another special appeal of the inro is its endless variety in subject and, most particularly, in technique. The display of the pieces in this exhibition easily reveals the diversity and varied beauty of the inro form as it developed during the long Tokugawa reign.

What *is* an inro? A device for carrying small objects by a people who had no pockets, it was a small nest of boxes skillfully fitted into one another and suspended by silk cords that pass through a sliding bead called the *ojime,* thence under the sash (*obi*), and at the top edge, held in place by a toggle called a *netsuke.* The *ojime* could be moved up the cords to allow the boxes of the inro to open or down to insure that the boxes stayed tightly closed. We call the inro a medicine box, but the literal translation of the word is "seal basket," suggesting that originally the inro was used for the carrying of personal seals and the accompanying ink pad. However, it is generally agreed that the main function of the inro as we know it became that of holding the patent medicines and drugs beloved of the Japanese. At first it was worn only by men of the upper classses, but as the nineteenth century advanced it was worn by anyone who could afford to buy so expensive an item— becoming, in effect, a kind of jewelry for people denied any personal adornment by Japan's strict sumptuary laws. Probably only rarely would it have been worn by women; for a time the many layers of the fashionable female costume would hardly allow it, and later the style of the very wide, tightly fitted female *obi* made its use impossible.

The history of the inro coincides, roughly, with the Momoyama and Tokugawa periods, about four hundred years. Its origin is murky, and the lack of documentary evidence and records of artists is frustrating to the student of lacquer. The first inro that is specifically known was owned by Hideyoshi and given to the abbot of the Kinkwan Temple about 1595, so the form must have originated some years before, probably during the early or mid-sixteenth century. With the opening of Japan and the Meiji era, and the accompanying rush to Western dress with its pockets, the use of the inro declined rapidly in the cities, more gradually in the hinterlands.

Casal, U. A. *Japanese Art Lacquers,* Sophia University, Tokyo, 1961.

While the viewer of the inro in this exhibition can appreciate their beauty and sheer decorative qualities, their wide range of colors and shadings, the variety of subject matter depicted, and the mechanical precision with which the cases fit together so that the covering design maintains an uninterrupted flow even while they are completely functional, not so obvious is the amount of time and infinite patience required to produce these effects.

An inro may have as many as sixty layers of lacquer (or more) from start to finish, each of which had to dry overnight or longer in a damp press (a box constantly covered with moist cloths), then ground to smoothness and polished before the next layer could similarly be applied, dried, and polished—a time-consuming process of weeks or months. The inro's base, or core, usually of wood, had to be prepared with extreme care and accuracy by a specialist called a joiner. Woods had to be thoroughly seasoned, and sometimes inro cores were suspended in the air for years, exposed to the vagaries of weather and temperature, so that no possible cracking or warping should ever occur. When the core was at last deemed fit, it was primed and covered with several layers of lacquer by a special class of workers called the *nurimono-shi* whose job was to prepare the core for the lacquer artist, known as the *makie-shi*. Dozens of steps were involved in applying these basic lacquer layers onto the wooden core before it was ready for decoration. Only then did the *makie-shi* begin his slow task of transferring his design onto the core and of repeated lacquerings, dustings, dryings, and polishings, until he was satisfied that he could do no more. Often he worked with other specialists in metalwork and inlay.

The evolution of the inro resulted in perhaps the finest miniature lacquer art ever seen, a utilitarian object of exquisite beauty that was highly prized, especially during the eighteenth and nineteenth centuries and again today. It is worthwhile to bear in mind some of the above considerations in viewing the finished products on display.

Virginia G. Atchley

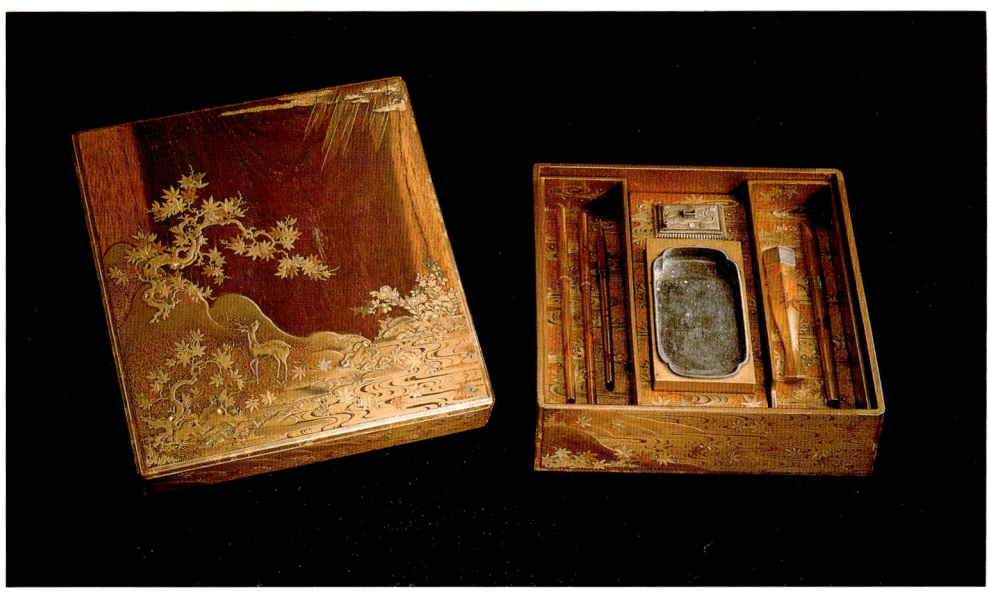

Suzuribako (writing box), cover and interior
18th c.

Design of deer and maple trees by hillside and stream, with gold and some silver *hiramakie* and *takamakie* on wood. Interior, complete with *mizuire,* inkstone, brushes (*fude*), and utensils, continues the design of maple leaves floating on water.

Below:
Same *suzuribako*

Showing inside of cover, with design of maple leaves and silver water drops along swirling stream in gold *togidashi* on rich *nashiji* ground.
From the collection of Etsuko and Joe Price

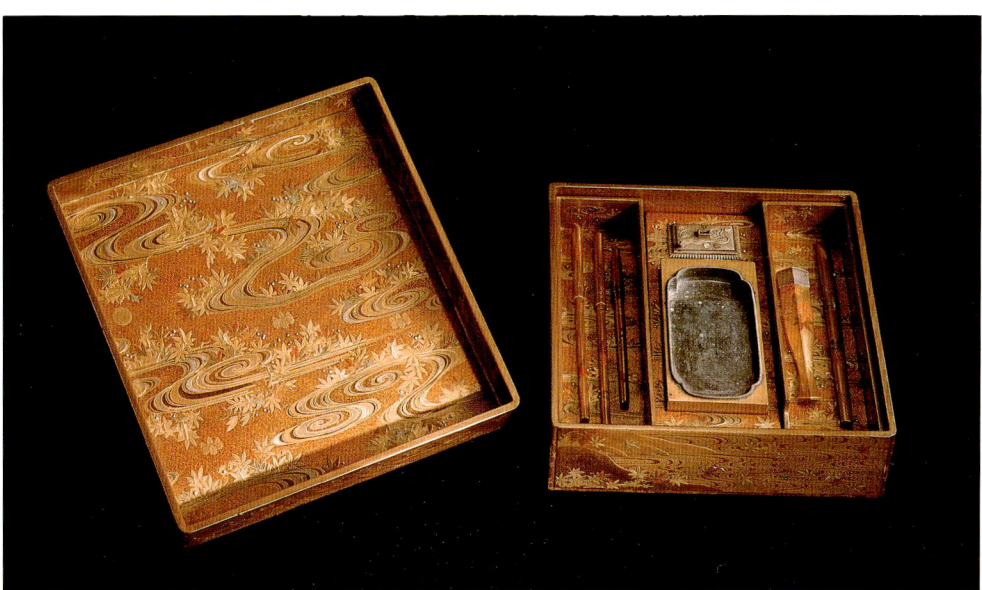

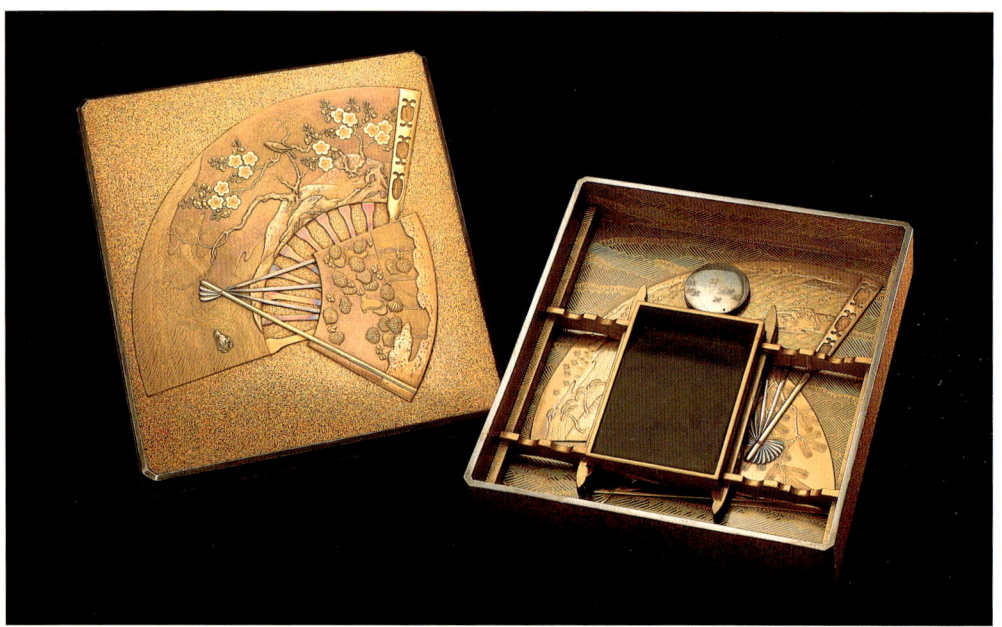

Suzuribako (writing box), cover and interior. Early 19th c.

Cover has design of decorated folding fans executed in gold and silver metal and *takamakie,* on a rich *nashiji* ground.

Interior is complete with silver water dropper (*mizuire*), inkstone (*suzuri*), and writing utensils, again on gold ground with fans.

Below: Same *suzuribako*

Showing inside of cover decorated with intricately designed fan, in gold and silver metal and *takamakie* on a gold lacquer wave-patterned ground.

From the collection of Etsuko and Joe Price

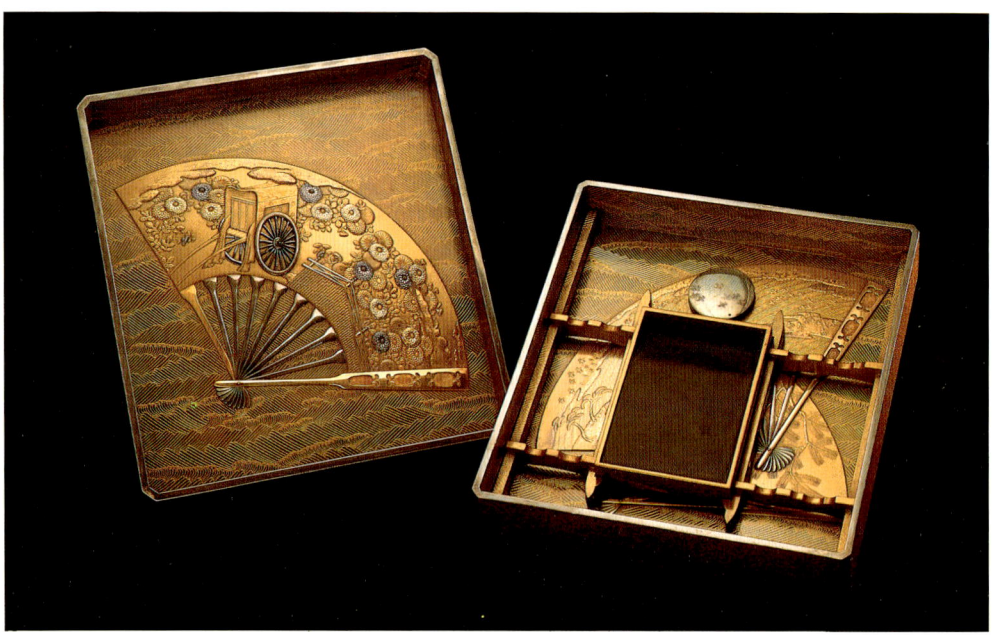

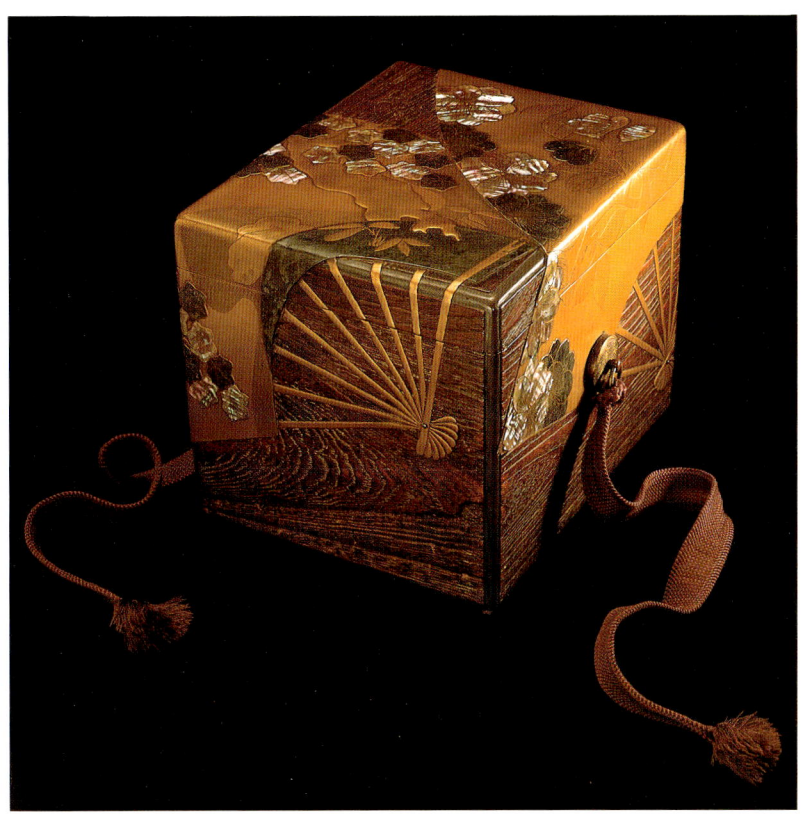

Large document box
(*bunko*)
19th c.

Decorated in Korin-style inlays of mother-of-pearl, pewter, and raised gold lacquers, on paulownia wood, with design of folding fans that sweep over top and sides.

Inside cover shows design of two geese on slightly raised gold lacquer flying across a full silver *togidashi* moon on a polished black *roiro* ground. From the collection of Etsuko and Joe Price

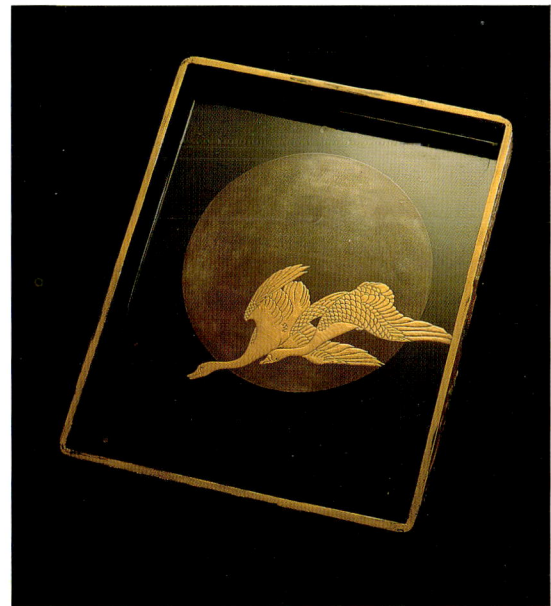

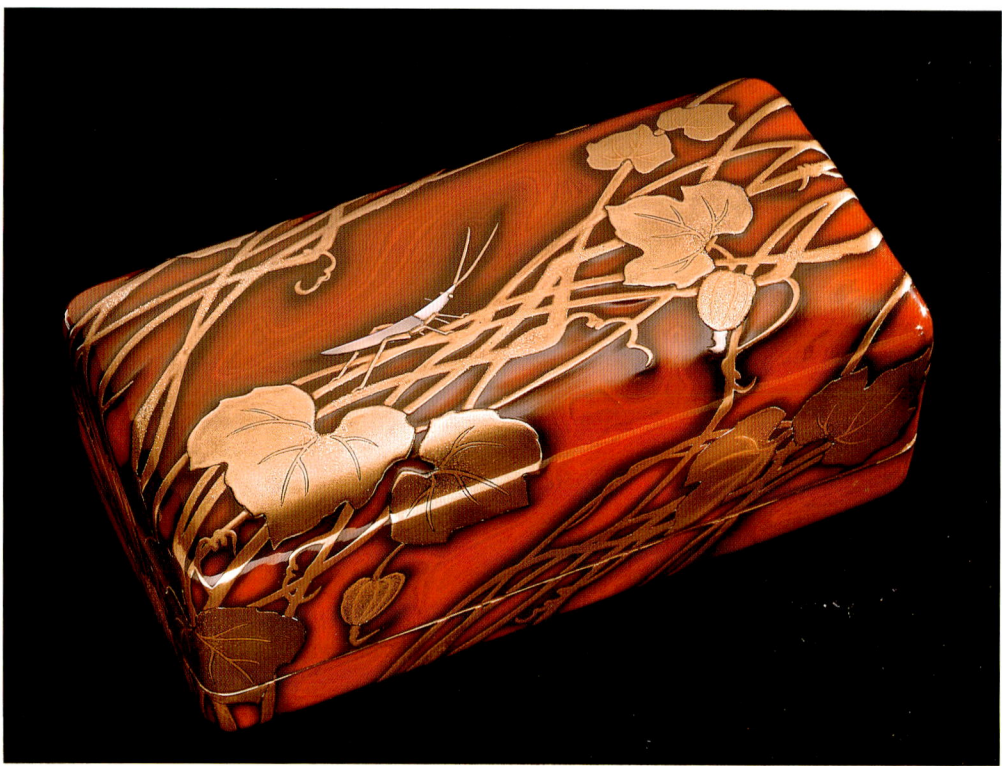

Tebako (cosmetic storage box)
Signed by the master lacquer *Showa* artist, *Mizuuchi (Misuuchi Kyohei, 1910–)* 20th c.

Depicting an insect on vines on a *mokume* ground and utilizing a combination of techniques in a very original and innovative manner. These techniques include a contemporary treatment of *tsuishu* (many-layered red lacquer), with the vines rendered in *takamakie* and *hiramakie* and the cricket inlaid in mother-of-pearl. The box is made of cypress wood.
From the collection of Bob and Elly Nordskog

Facing page:
Cosmetic box with tray and cover. 19th c.

Cover design shows boats and island in a body of water along a rocky coastline with Mt. Fuji in the distance. All in gold *takamakie* of varying thickness with *kirikane* against a *kinji* gold sky, and *nashiji* ground. Tray carries view of a temple on a hill, with trees in various shades of gold lacquer against dark outline of mountains, a gold *torii* at lower right edge.
From the collection of Etsuko and Joe Price

Fubako (letter box). Late 19th c.

Natural wood with gold lacquer and inlaid shell in the form of a bridge over a pond with irises.
From the collection of Etsuko and Joe Price

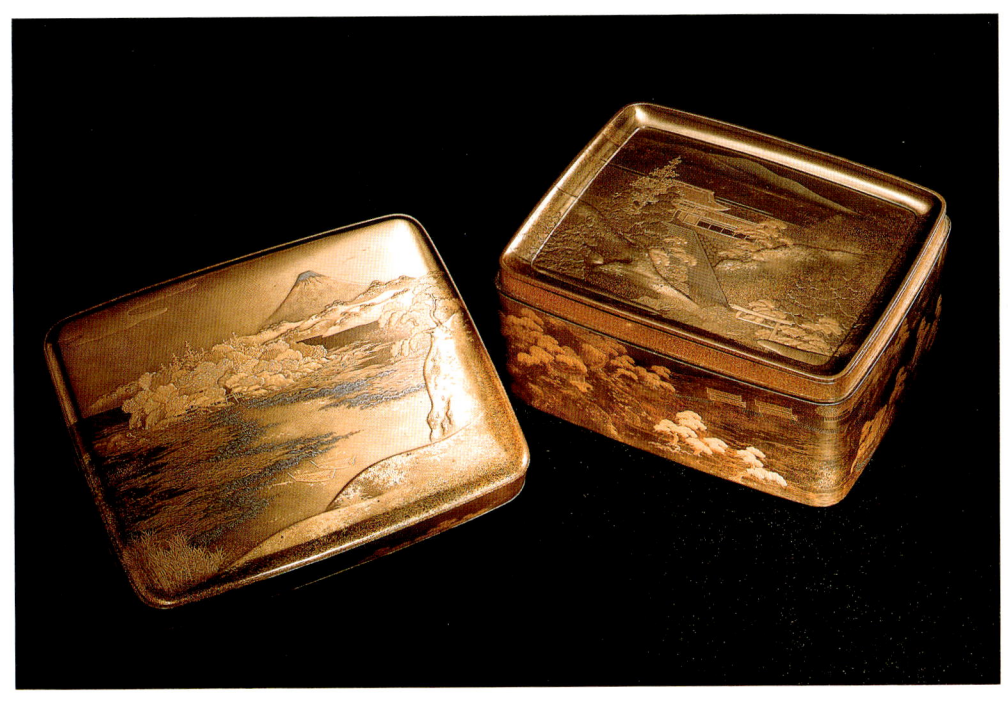

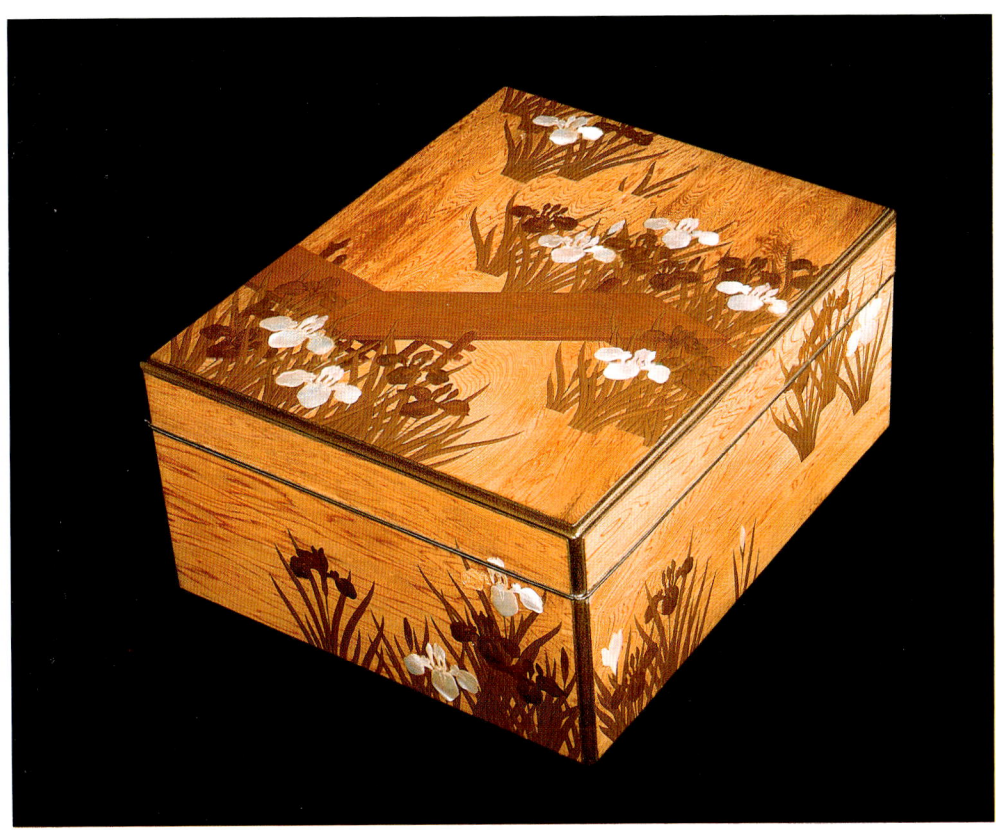

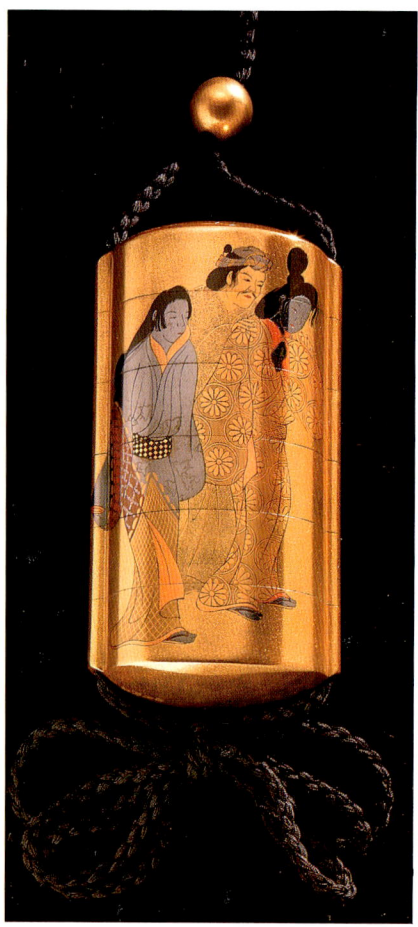

Five-case inro
Signed: *Tatsuke Takamasu*, late 18th–early 19th c.

Kinji ground, decoration in gold, silver, and polychrome *togidashi;* details in *kirikane* and *koban*. Compartments, risers, and rims in *fundame.* Depicting a moustached client wearing a type of turban entering the Fushiwara house, with a young courtesan and an older companion. Their robes of patterned red, silver and gold. The reverse shows an older woman with two Samurai swords, pointing the way to the entry. Her robe is patterned in silver and gold.
Ojime: Gold lacquer
From the collection of Bob and Elly Nordskog

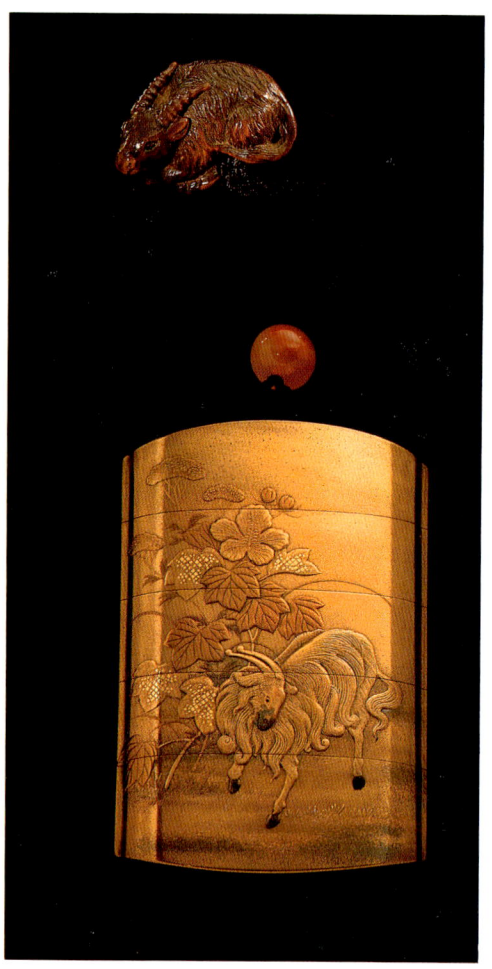

Four-case inro
By *Toyo (Kanshosai),* late 18th c.

Depicting a single goat with flower and leaves. The reverse has two goats under a tree, all executed in low *takamakie* on a *fundame* (dull gold) ground. Of the pair of goats, one is in gold, the other in pewter colored lacquer. The style shows Chinese influence (the position of head and body, together with the slender hoof is reminiscent of the Chinese style of painting grazing horses).
INTERIOR: *nashiji*
Ojime: Carnelian
Netsuke: Wooden reclining goat. Signed *Kokei.*
From the collection of Bob and Elly Nordskog

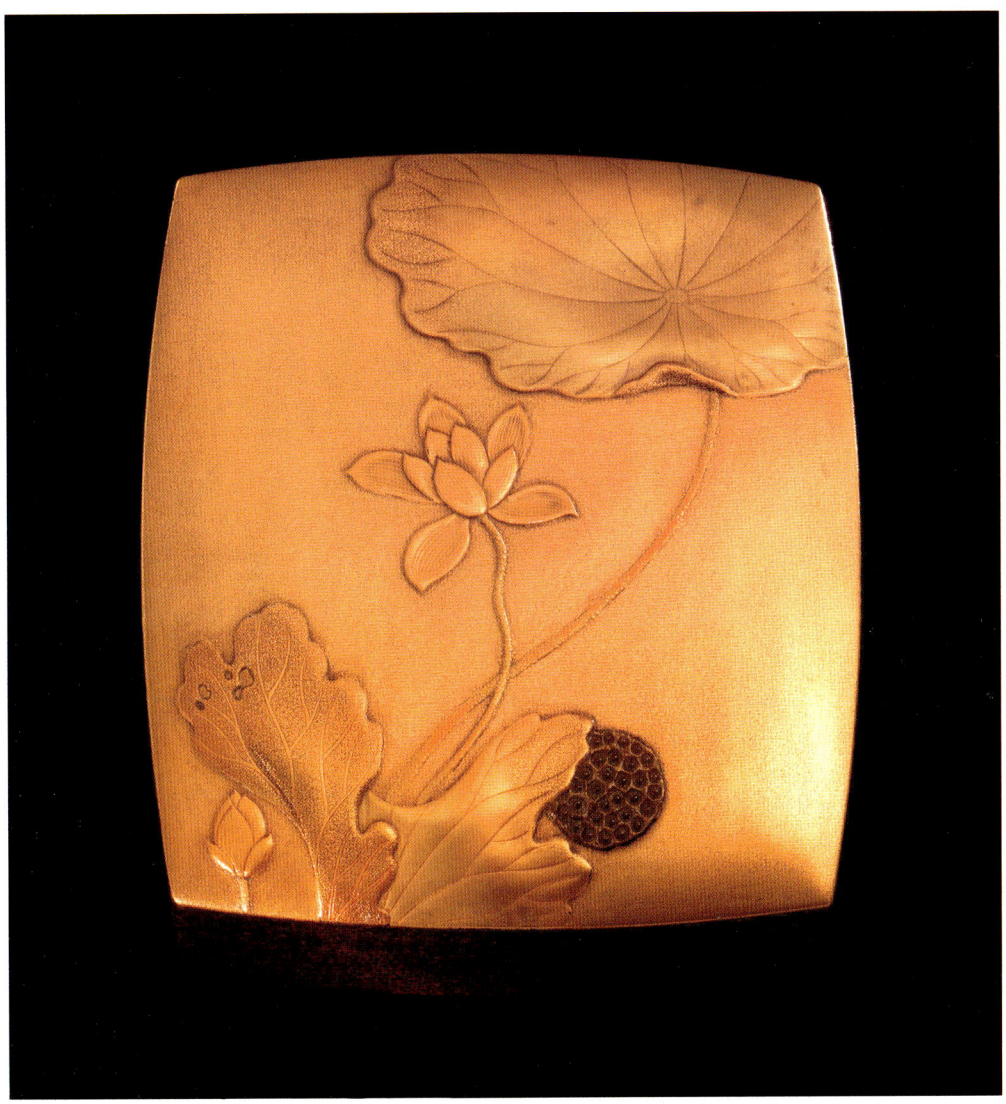

Box (*kogo*)
19th c.

Decorated in gold and silver lacquer with lotus flower design, with *nashiji* decorated sides. The inside lid with a small carved and lacquered frog.
From the collection of Bob and Elly Nordskog

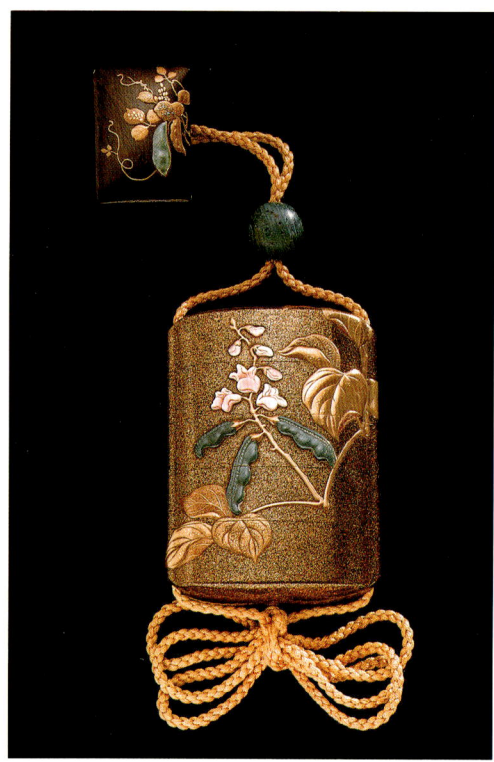

**Four-case inro
Unsigned: 19th c.**

Hiramakie, aogai, and stained ivory inlaid on a total *nashiji* ground. Design with grasshopper; reverse flowers in mother-of-pearl with green stained ivory beans. Golden leaves with some *kirigane* inlay.
INTERIOR: *nashiji*
Ojime: malachite bead
Netsuke: in the form of a *hako* lacquered and inlaid with pottery and shell in the form of peapods, tendrils, and leaves. Unsigned.
From the collection of Bob and Elly Nordskog

Shibayama sheath inro, 19th c.

Sheath, curved shape in bright gold *kinji* ground finely decorated in *shibayama* technique with two *oni* playing under the moon (one beating a skull)—one *oni* body rust color, the other flesh color. The reverse with a *ho-o* bird in silver and colored enamels surrounded by flowers (peonies and wisteria) all in coral and mother-of-pearl. Two *oni* ivory inlay. Three-case inro, on *Kinji* ground decorated with four roundels (two on each side) of birds and flowers design in *takamakie*.
INTERIOR: *nashiji*
Ojime: Coral
Netsuke: Lacquer *manju* of bright *kinji* with *hozuki* (winter cherries) in *hiramakie* with center inlaid coral. The *hozuki* bud is an inlay in pure gold. Signed *Kajikawa.* 19th c.
From the collection of Bob and Elly Nordskog

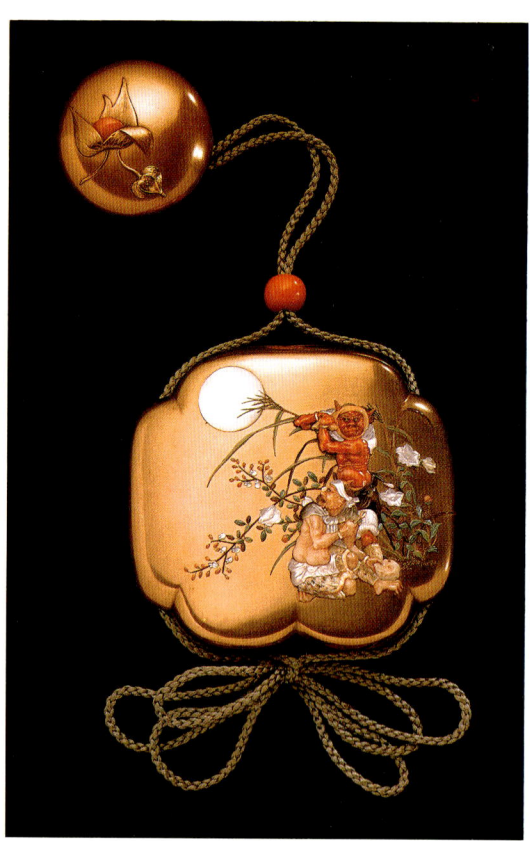

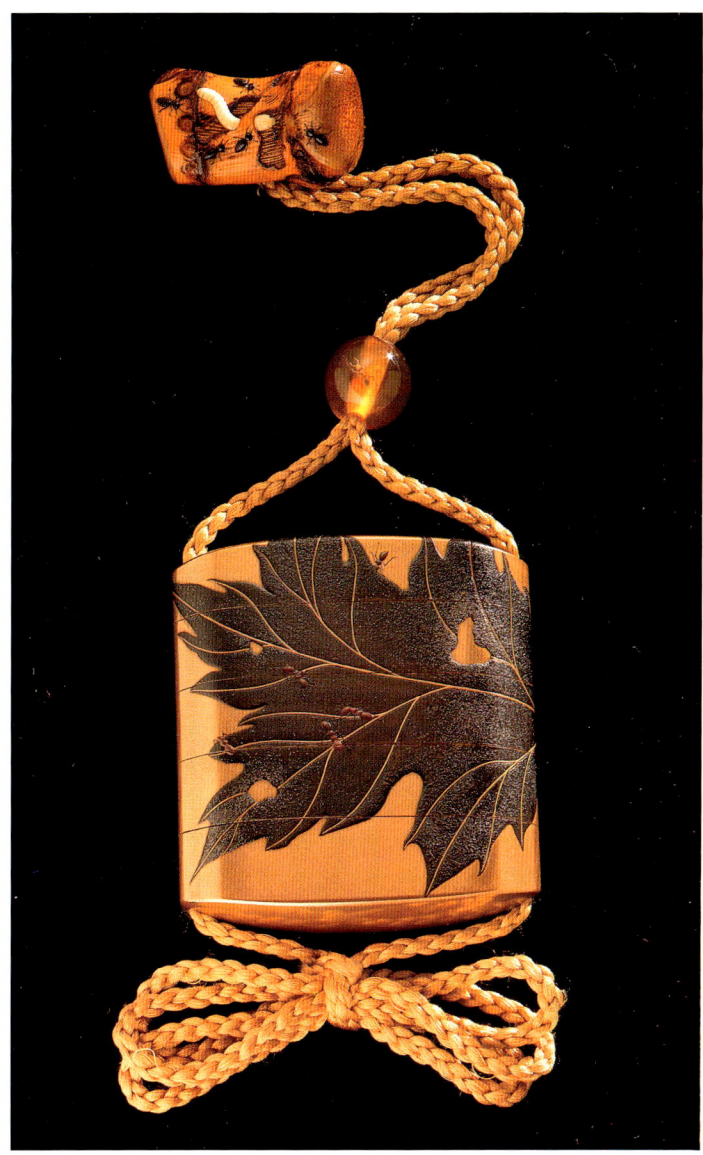

Four-case inro
Signed *Zeshin* on bottom in typical scratched signature (*Shibata Zeshin* 1807–1891)

Kinji (bright gold) ground with a black *ishime* mulberry leaf covering the front, with gold veining and five brown lacquer ants crawling over it. The reverse with attached gold cocoons bulging with silkworms and three brown ants crawling on them.
Ojime: Amber with ants caught inside. Gold ant decoration.
netsuke: Carved bamboo root, ivory grub with lacquered eyes and black lacquered ants.
From the collection of Bob and Elly Nordskog.

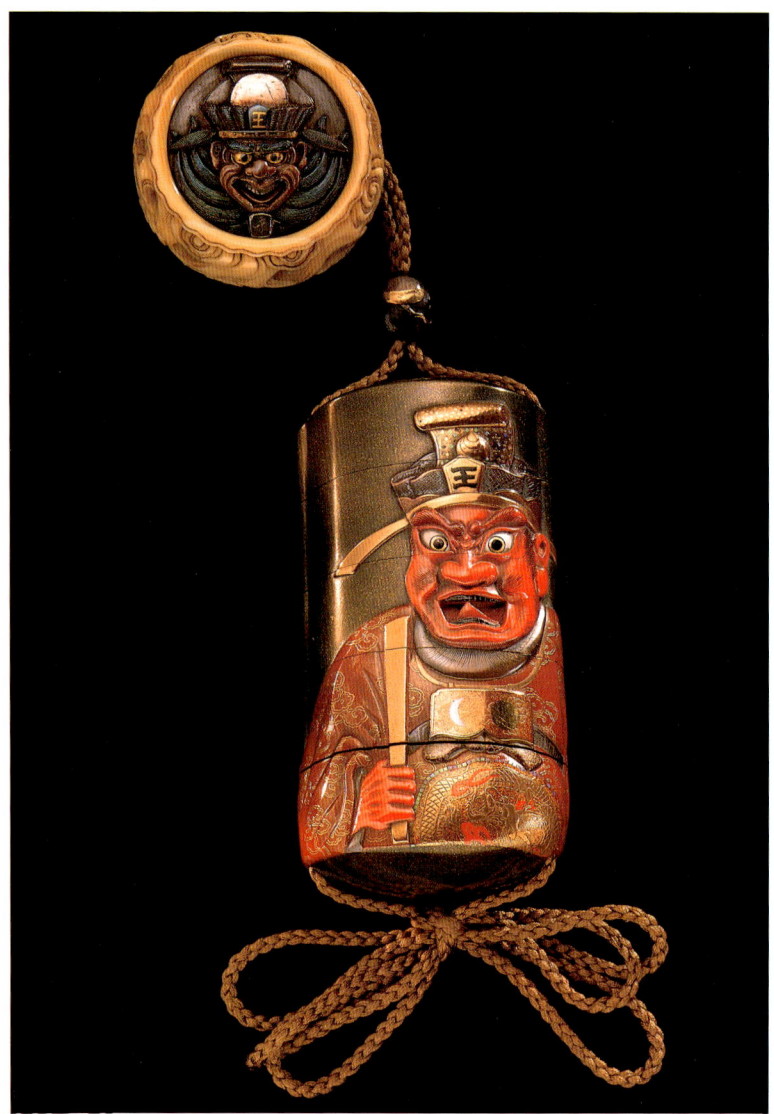

Four-case inro
Signed: *Joka*

Dark green ground with *"Emma-O,"* the King of Hell, in red and gold *hiramakie,* and with inlaid eyes holding his sword and wearing his hat with the usual sign for *Emma-O.* The reverse with a nose and eyeball on a red lacquer stand.
INTERIOR: *nashiji*
Ojime: Bronze inlaid with gold and silver in the form of a fruiting branch.
Netsuke: Kagamibuta — metal disk in the form of *Emma-O,* silver inlaid with copper and several colors of gold, the marine ivory bowl pierced and carved in the form of Buddhist symbols in clouds. Unsigned.
From the collection of Bob and Elly Nordskog

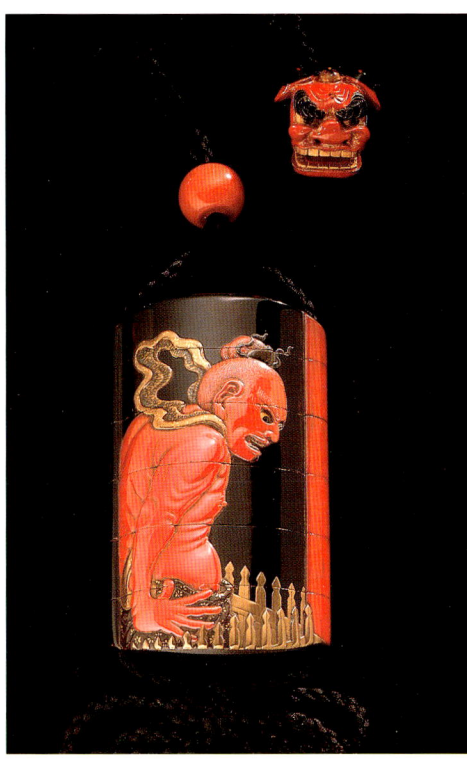

Five-case inro
Signed: *Jitokusai Gyokuzan* with *kakihan.* Late 18th c.

A bold and powerful *Nio* and a fence with the pagoda of the temple guarded by a *Nio* on the reverse. Finely rendered with dramatic originality in red *takamakie* in high relief with details in gold on a high-polish *roiro* ground. Scenes on the reverse delicately rendered in *togidashi.*
INTERIOR: *nashiji* and *fundame.*
Ojime: Coral
Netsuke: Shishimai, with articulated jaw, in wood with red, black, and gold lacquer. Unsigned.
From the collection of Bob and Elly Nordskog

Three-case inro
Unsigned. Attributed to *Gyokuzan* or the *Komo Kansai* family. Ca 1830

Decorated in thick *takamakie* techniques with *Daruma,* his eyes inlaid, on a dark green ground, decorated in red and gold. Across the lower part of the design, and extending to the reverse, is a floral spray, perhaps of prunus. The case interiors are decorated.
Ojime: Copper *Daruma* with silver inlaid eyes
Netsuke: Carved and lacquered wood in the form of two *Darumas* seated on a fly whisk. Signed.
From the collection of Bob and Elly Nordskog

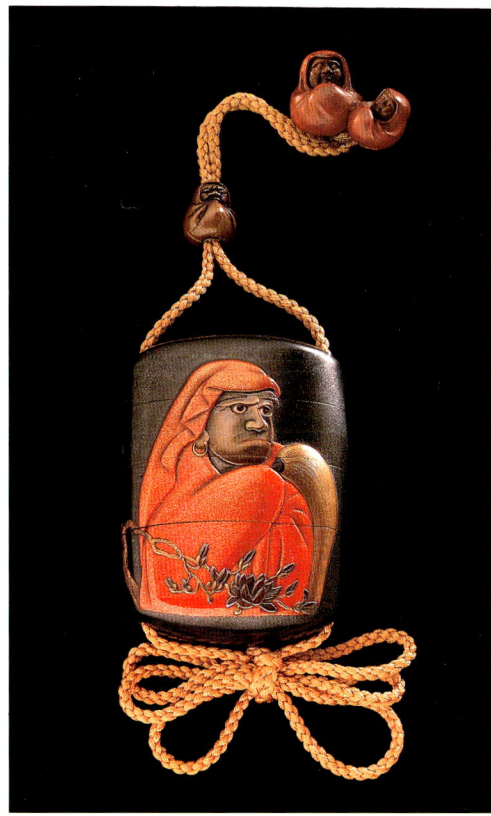

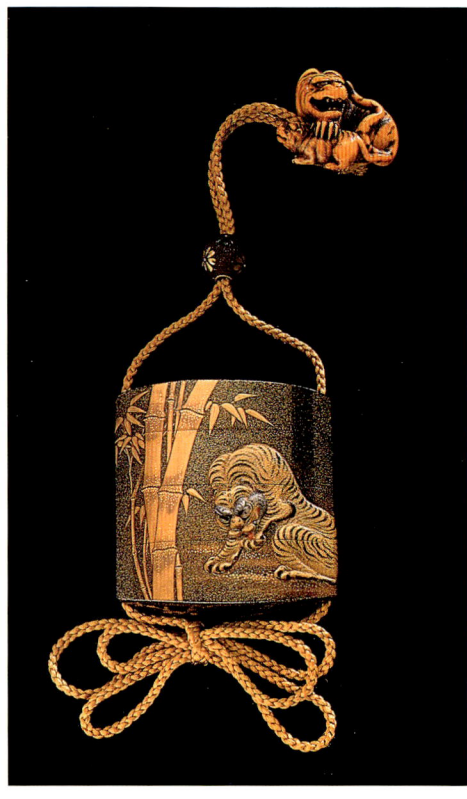

Three-case inro
Signed: *Toyo* with *kakihan*.
18th–19th c.

Decorated with a tiger whose tail wraps around the reverse side, and bamboo trees. *Takamakie* and *hiramakie* on *roiro* ground, with sparse *nashiji,* accented with *kirigane.*
INTERIOR: *fundame*
Ojime: Metal, inlaid with copper, silver, and gold chrysanthemums
Netsuke: Ivory tiger and cub, the eyes inlaid with horn. Signed *Hakuryu*
From the collection of Bob and Elly Nordskog

Five-case inro
Signed: *Koma Kyuhaku saku*. Late 18th c.

Depicting two butterflies and falling leaves rendered in blue/black *takamakie* with mother-of-pearl inlay on an unusual rich red lacquer ground with delicately sprinkled *kinpun.*
INTERIOR: *nashiji*
Ojime: Wood, lacquered in the design of butterflies, shell inlay
Netsuke: Lacquered wood in the form of butterfly dancer with the face inlaid with ivory, hair ornaments inlaid with ivory and shell. Unsigned.
From the collection of Bob and Elly Nordskog

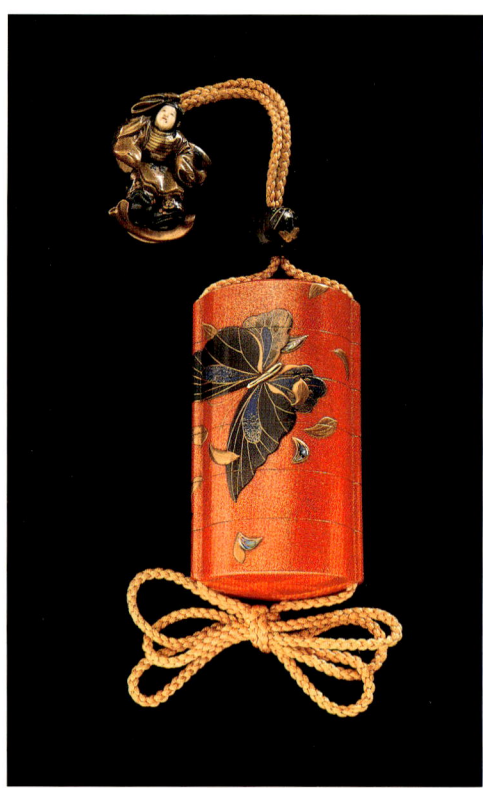

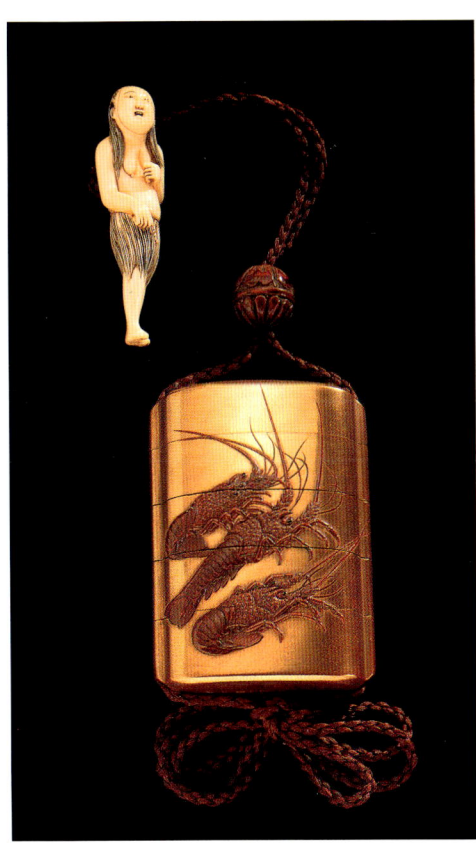

Hinged case with silver hinge and lock. 18th c.

Black lacquer, decorated on one side with blue ceramic bird on a branch; the reverse shows a deep red lacquer coxcomb flower, inlaid with lacquer and shell.

From the collection of Bob and Elly Nordskog

Four-case inro
Signed: *Chohei saku,* early 19th c.

Gold (*fundame*) ground with *takamakie* crayfish in dark red lacquer. Three fish on one side, two on other.
Ojime: Carved lacquer
Netsuke: 18th c. ivory *ama* (fisher-girl). Unsigned.
From the collection of Bob and Elly Nordskog

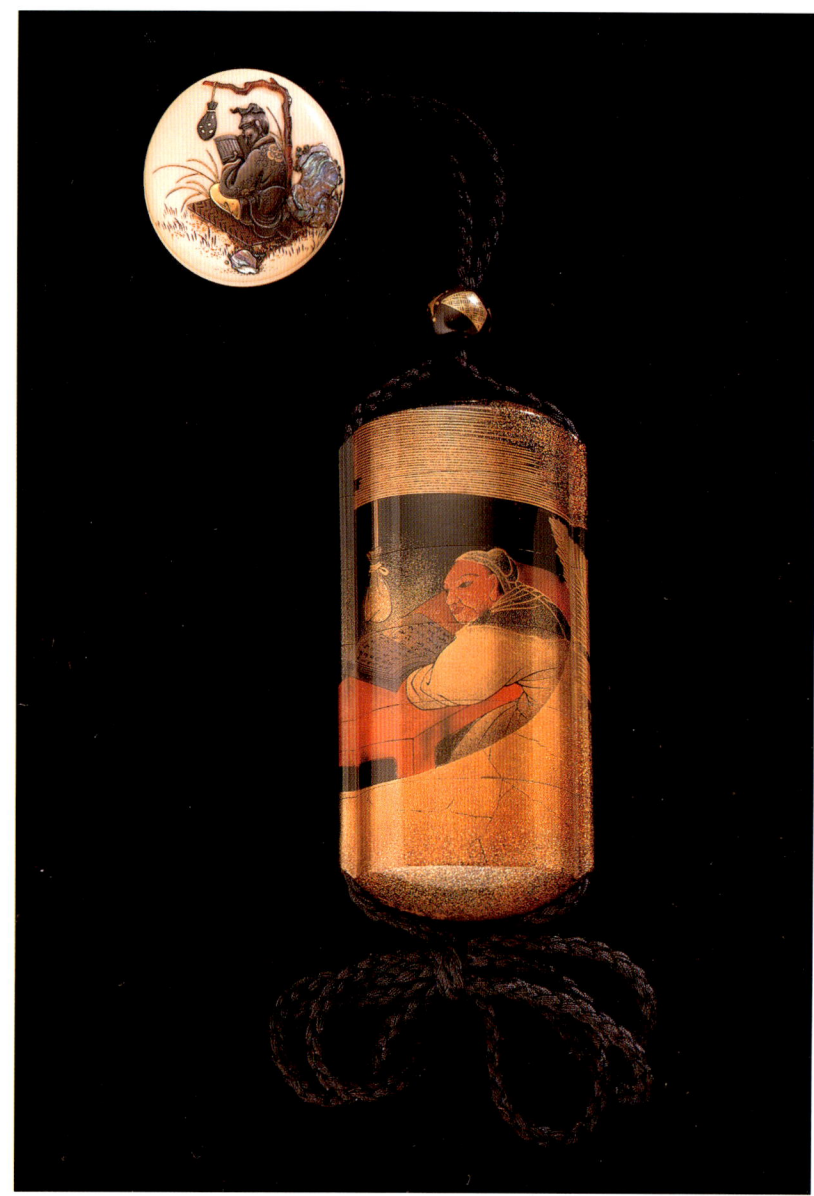

Five-case inro
Signed: *Toyo saku,* early 19th c.

Togidashi and *nashiji* ground depicting a poor scholar reading by the only light he had, a bag of fireflies. The student sitting outside his window in colors of red and gold. The reverse with palm fronds at lower portion of inro.

INTERIOR: *nashiji*

Ojime: Bronze with gold lacquer decoration of brocade patterns.
Netsuke: Ivory *manju* inlaid with metal, shell, tortoiseshell, and horn, with the same theme as the inro. Signed.

From the collection of Bob and Elly Nordskog

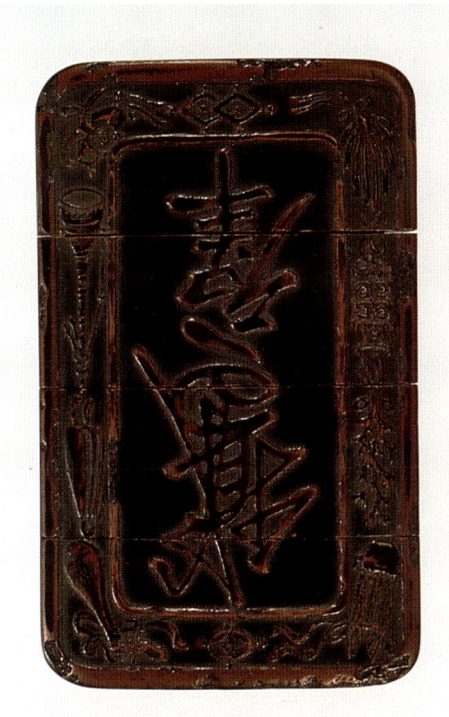

Three-case inro
Signed on bottom: *Ritsuo* (1663–1747). Probably genuine.

Design in black lacquer of old inkstick with musical instruments and other objects around edge. Two large characters in center.
INTERIOR: black lacquer, shoulders and rims in *fundame*.
Ojime: grooved cylindrical wood bead
Netsuke: Manju in shape of *kagamibuta;* scalloped and black-lacquered bowl around design of young ferns and bracken (*warabi*) shoots, in pewter and mother-of-pearl, on *ishime* ground. Signed Issai, 19th c.

Same three-case inro

Reverse shows ferns (*warabi*) inlaid in pewter, gold and green pottery, and mother-of-pearl.
From the collection of Virginia and Raymond Atchley

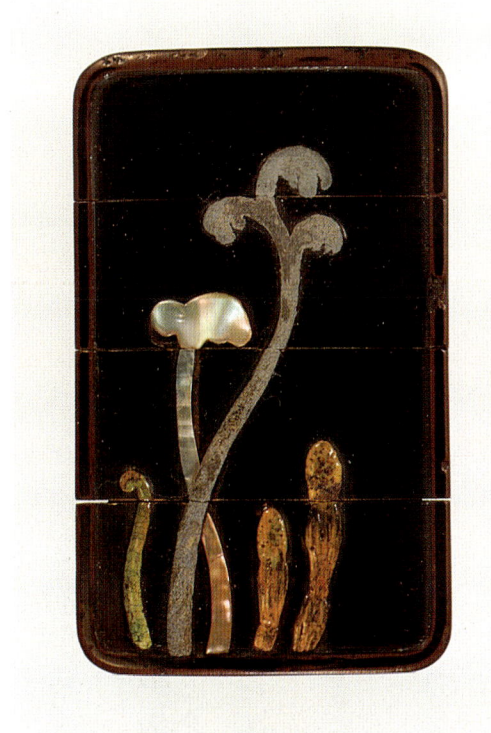

19

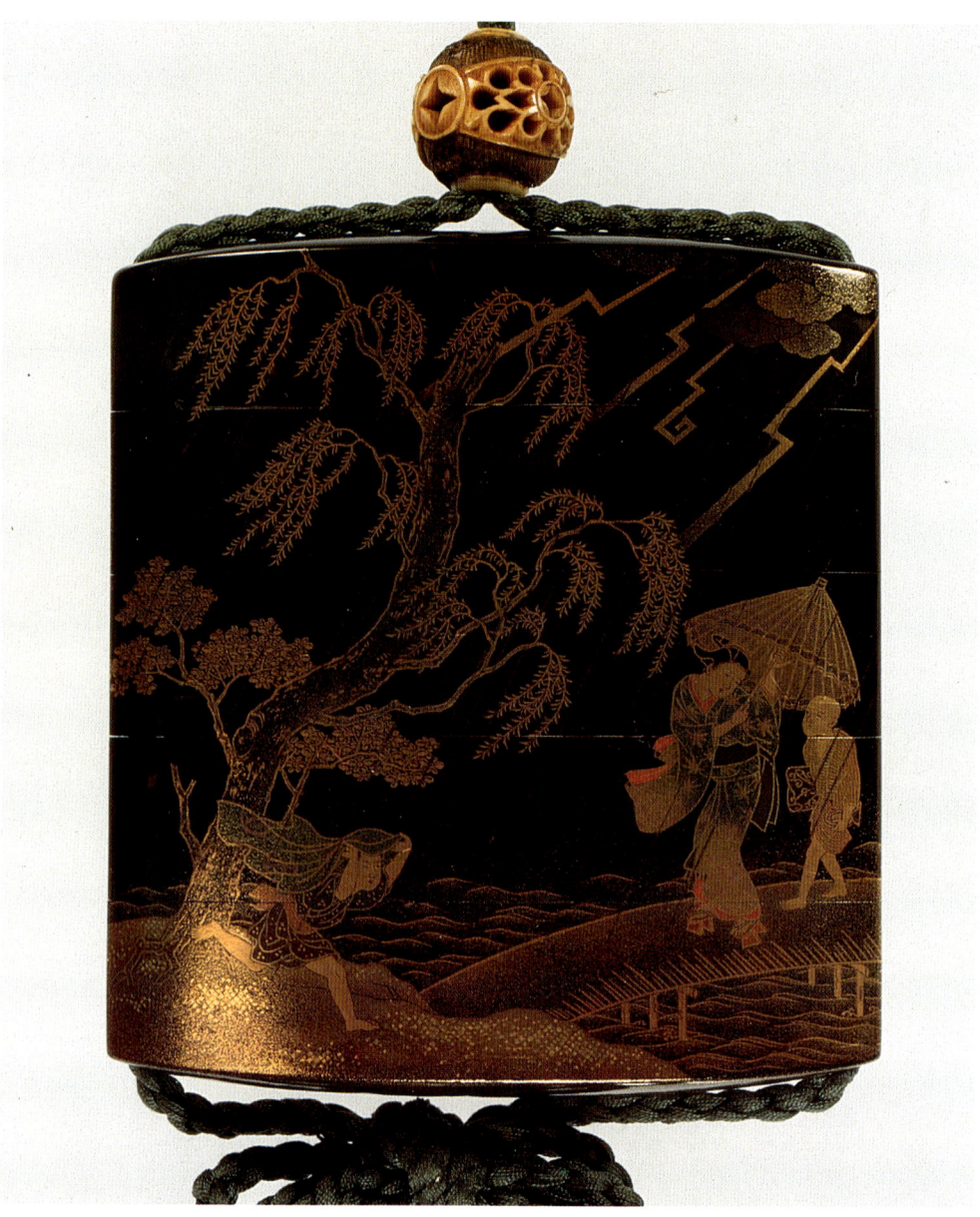

Four-case inro
Signed: *Kanshosai,* with *kakihan.* 18th c.

Design, which flows around both sides of the inro, is in *ukiyo-e* style (copied from a print by *Sukenobu*) and shows a group of courtesans and companions caught in a sudden, wind-whipped thunderstorm and scurrying for cover from the slanting rain. Executed in *togidashi,* with gold, *koban,* black and colored lacquers, with some *kirikane,* on polished *roiro* ground. The kimonos, in soft vari-colored lacquer, are covered with delicate gold patterns, and the wall of the temple under the eaves of which they seek shelter is in *mokume* technique. All the interior is gold *fundame.*
Ojime: carved staghorn
Netsuke: manju-kagamibuta type: stag-antler bowl with gold lacquer; lid is stained green stag-antler with gold lacquer flower design. Unsigned.

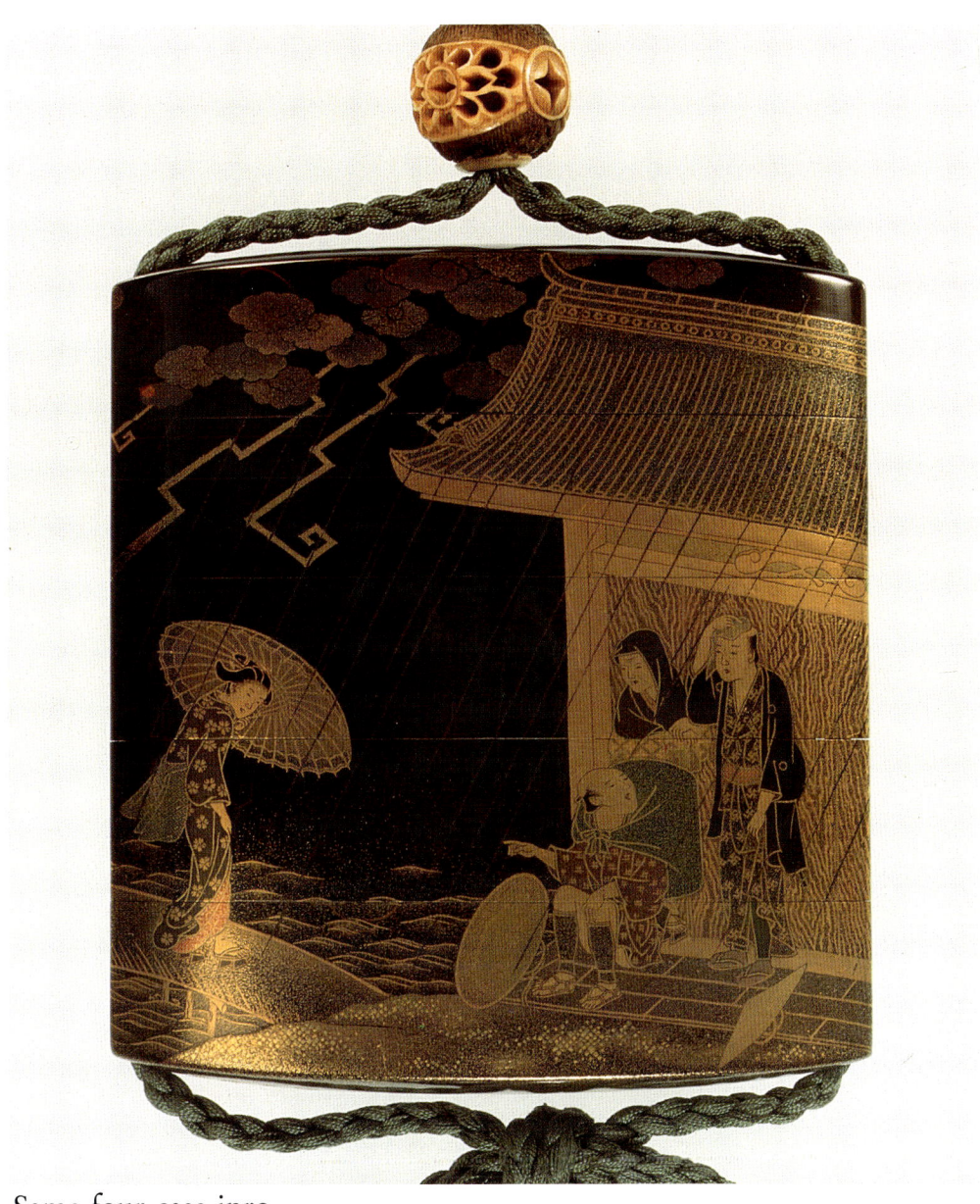

Same four-case inro

Reverse shows continuation from the design of *Sukenobu's* print
From the collection of Virginia and Raymond Atchley

Miniature three-case inro
Unsigned. 19th c.

On an *ishime* dark-brown lacquer ground, design of a large lotus blossom inset in mother-of-pearl, lotus leaves inlaid in simulated pewter and *takamakie* brown lacquer, with thin gold stems and flecks of *aogai*. Design runs over top.
INTERIOR: black lacquer; bottom case inset with silver.
Ojime: very small silver, with design of two flying heron.
Netsuke: small mother-of-pearl *manju*. Unsigned.

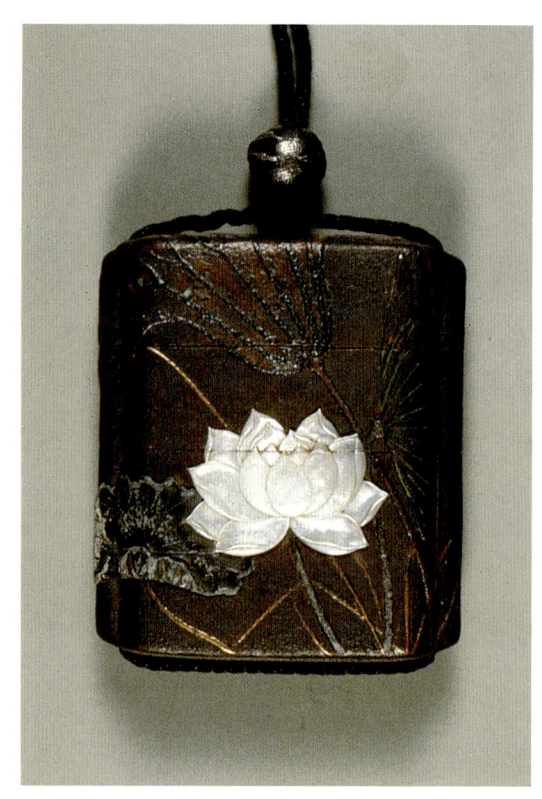

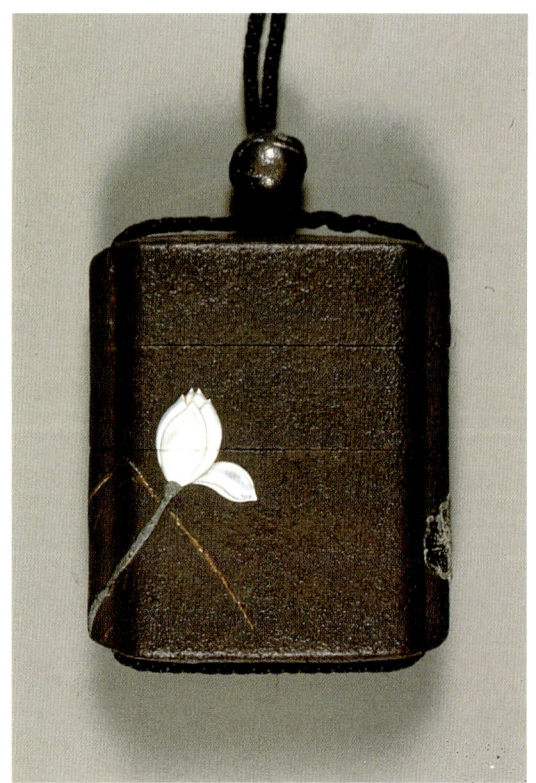

Same miniature three-case inro

Reverse shows single lotus bud in mother-of-pearl.
From the collection of Virginia and Raymond Atchley

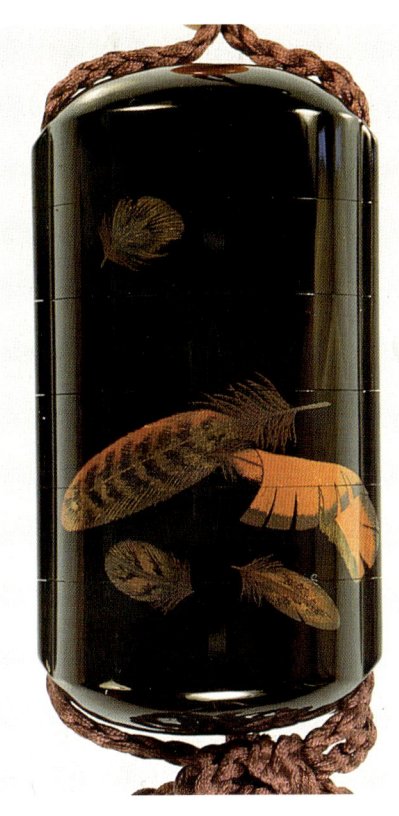

Five-case inro
Signed: *Shunsui* with red lacquer *kakihan*. Early 19th c.

Togidashi, with design of scattered pheasant feathers in gold, silver, and orange-red lacquer on highly polished *roiro* ground.
INTERIOR: rich red-gold *nashiji* throughout.
Ojime: coral
Netsuke: two-piece *manju,* black-lacquered wood with two oak leaves in gold *hiramakie;* reverse covered with *sosho* calligraphy in gold *hiramakie.* Signed, on front, *Jokasai.*

Same five-case inro
Reverse shows more floating pheasant feathers.
From the collection of Virginia and Raymond Atchley

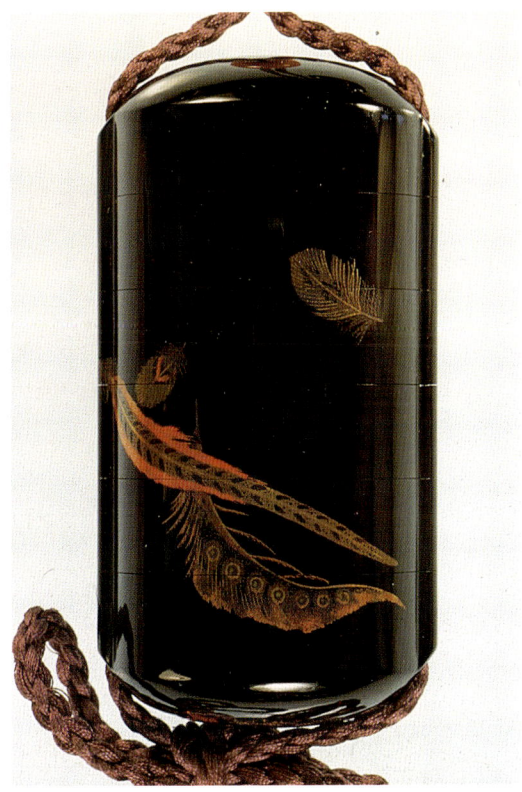

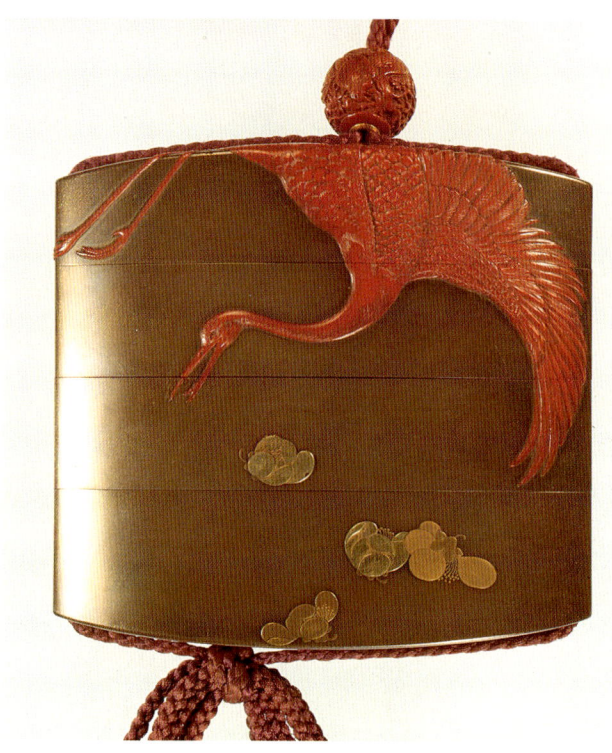

Three-case inro
Signed: *Kajikawa Tomohide (Chuei) saku*, with *kakihan*.
18th–19th c.

Decorated on the *rogin* ground (soft silver-brown with faintest sprinkling of finest gold dust) with a *tsuishu* crane flying among floating plum blossoms in gold lacquer and gold leaf, the design continuing over the top onto the reverse.
INTERIOR: red lacquer; risers in *nashiji*, with the rims and shoulders in *fundame*.

Ojime: deeply carved *tsuishi* rooster and hen among wheat sheaves and flowering shrubs, on diapered ground.
Netsuke: delicate wood *haku* with cover design of long-necked heron in gold *hiramakie*, with red-lac seal reading "after a design by (Sakai) *Hoitsu.*" Signed *Gyokuzan.*

Same three-case inro

Reverse shows continuation of design. From the collection of Virginia and Raymond Atchley

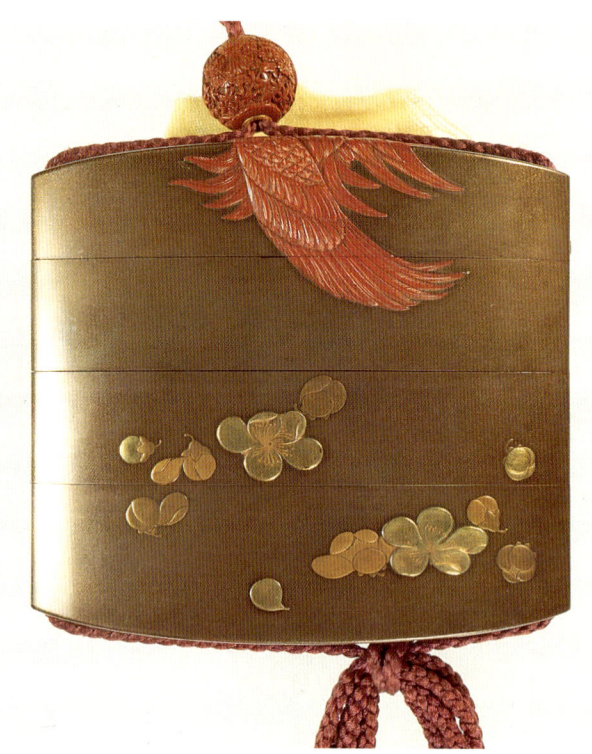

Four-case inro, "Koma" shape
Signed: *Koma Ankyo saku* (Koma III, died 1715). Also known as *Koma Yasumasa* and *Kyuhaku I*.

Two prancing horses (one on each side) in slightly raised *takamakie* on beige-brown lacquer ground (*rogin*). One horse is in orange lacquer with gold mane, tail, and fetlocks, and black hooves and muzzle.
INTERIOR: divided compartments in orange lacquer, risers in black lacquer, rims and shoulders in *fundame*.

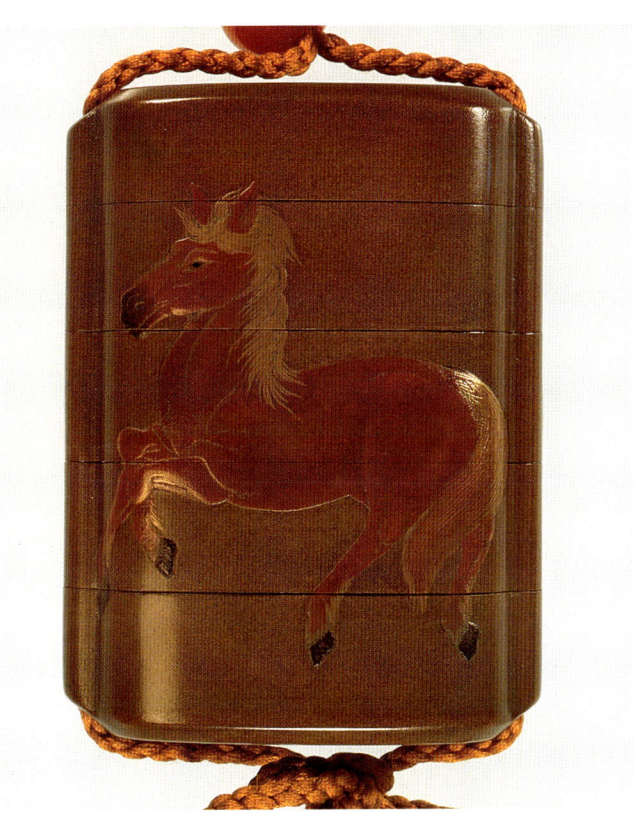

Ojime: hardstone
Netsuke: wood standing horse. Unsigned.

Same four-case inro, "Koma" shape

Reverse shows horse in black lacquer sprinkled with fine gold dust, and with gold mane, tail, and fetlocks.
From the collection of Virginia and Raymond Atchley

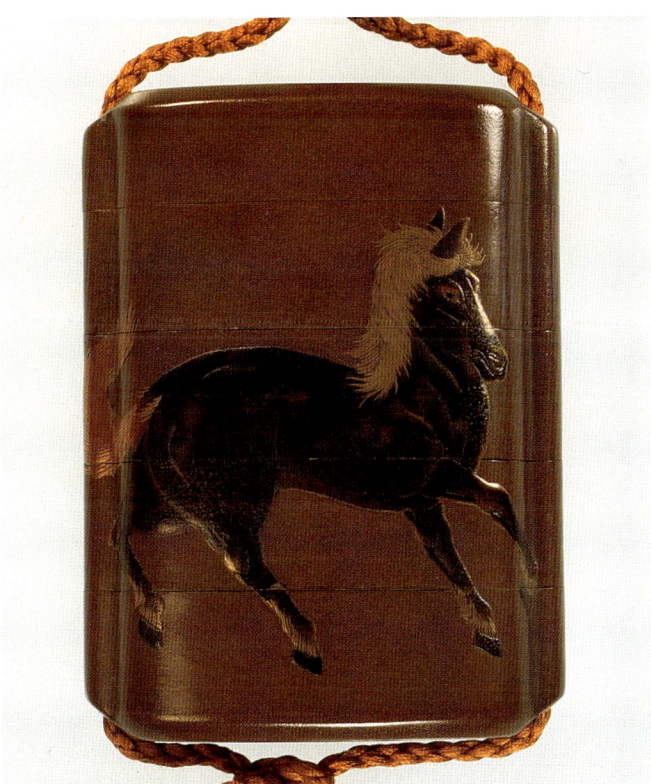

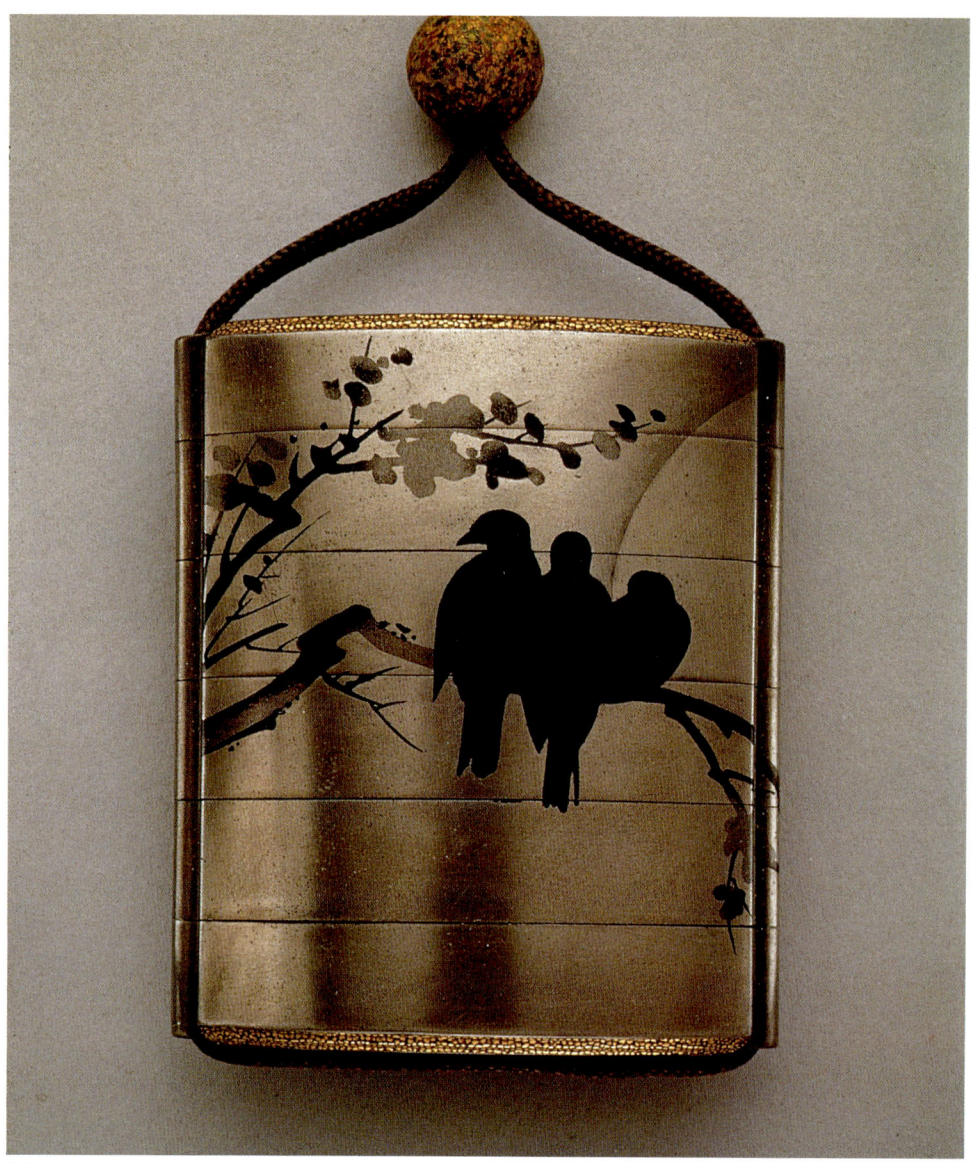

Five-case inro
Signed: "*Toju* at the age of 70," with red *kakihan*

Design, in *sumie-togidashi* on silver ground, of very black crows, seated on flowering branches before a large silver moon. (Design taken from a Korin painting.) The silvery lacquer ground is remarkably metallic-looking. Top and bottom are flat silver, and there is a ridged line of *gyobu* between the *joge* and sides.
INTERIOR: Risers are bright *nashiji* with *fundame* shoulders and rims. Each case contains a tight-fitting silver metal container with a rectangular strip of gold on the cover for writing name of drug it contains. The risers are shaped with a shallow cutout in the center so that the container boxes can be removed.
Ojime: Oblong silver with black crow in *shakudo*.
Netsuke: Kagamibuta, dark wood case, with a silver plate decorated with three crows on branch of withered tree. Unsigned.
From the collection of Virginia and Raymond Atchley

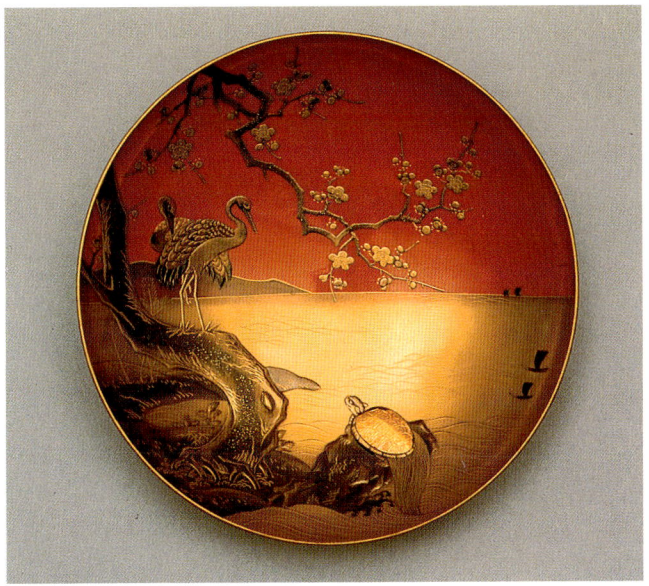

Sakazuki (sake cup set)
early 19th c.
(One of a set of three)

Decorated with symbols of good fortune and longevity (probably a wedding set) of *minogame*, crane, bamboo, pine tree, and plum — all in gold and black *takamakie* on a red and gold ground.
From the collection of Virginia and Raymond Atchley

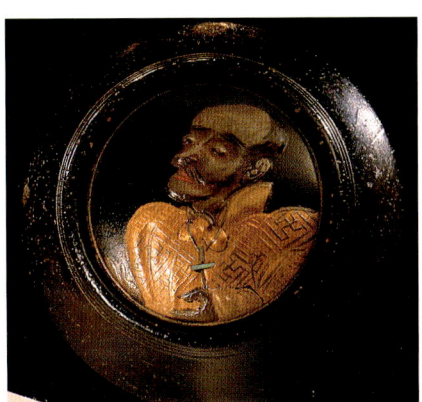

Netsuke

Kagamibuta with a multi-colored lacquered metal disk in the design of a Portuguese man wearing a cross inlaid in shell. The bowl is dark wood. Unsigned.
From the collection of Bob and Elly Nordskog

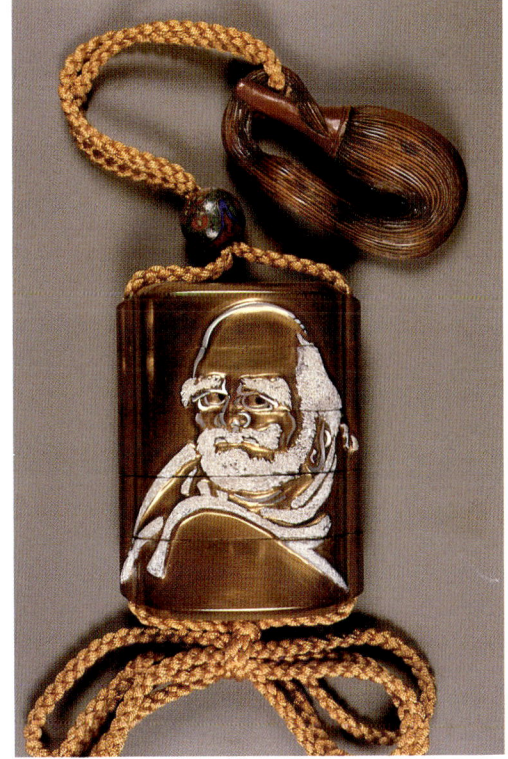

Four-case inro
Unsigned. 19th c.

Large raised design of Daruma's head outlined in oxidized pewter and mother-of-pearl on solid *kinji* ground. Reverse has design of swaying tree fronds similarly outlined.
INTERIOR: red-gold *gyobu nashiji*, with *fundame* shoulders and rims.
Ojime: ivory seated *Daruma*
Netsuke: wood and lacquer *hossu*, unsigned.
From the collection of Virginia and Raymond Atchley

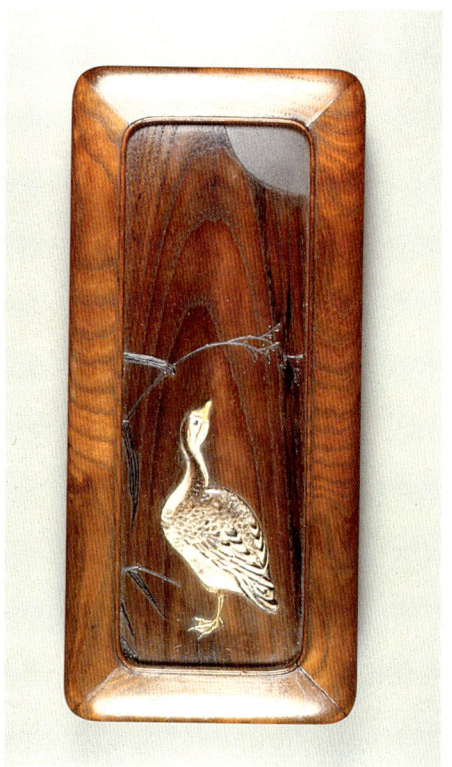

Suzuribako (writing box)
Early 20th c.

Small oblong writing box of beautifully grained wood (mulberry) with pottery by *Kenya* (attested by *tomobako*), lacquer by *Taishin,* as signed on inside of cover.

   The cover design, in a beveled frame, shows a goose in grey, white, and yellow pottery, his head uplifted to gaze at the corner of a full grey-lacquer moon in the upper righthand corner. Just a suggestion of grasses and leaves in same dark grey lacquer. On inside cover again the merest suggestion of a swirling stream in silver-grey *togidashi.* Signed *Taishin* in gold.

   Small *mizuire* with design of chrysanthemums and leaves in thick gold and silver metal on a *nanako* ground. From the collection of Virginia and Raymond Atchley

Tray (*bon*), in lacquered wood. Unsigned. 19th c.

The dark grey lacquered ground is decorated with an *inro* and a *kozuka.* The inro, en suite with gold *ojime* and gold rabbit *netsuke*, all in high *takamakie,* carries a design of two silver herons in *togidashi* on a matte black ground with sprinkled *nashiji,* cords in dark brown lacquer. The *kozuka* handle is matte black lacquer with designs of birds, pine needles, and nets in fine-line gold lacquer imitating *hirazogan.* The *kozuka* blade is silver lacquer.

From the collection of Virginia and Raymond Atchley

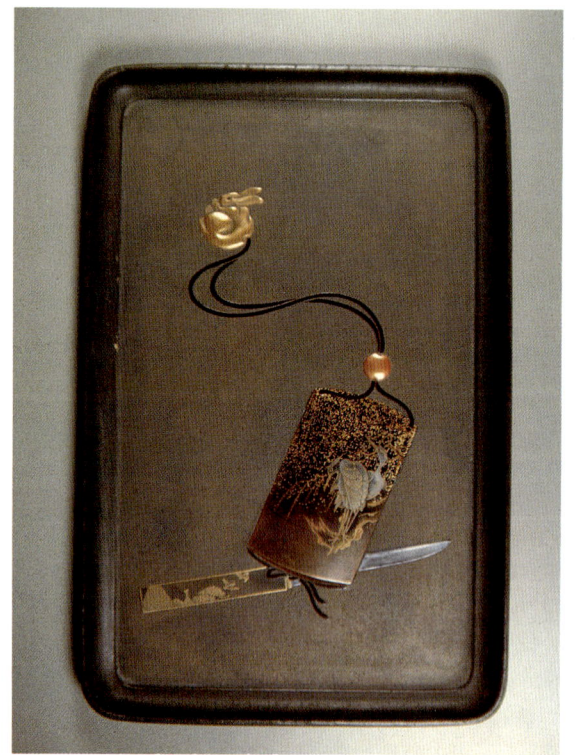

GLOSSARY
(Lacquer techniques in italics)

abumi	stirrup
aogai	shavings of iridescent pearl shell. (Often used synonymously with *somada* and *raden*)
aoi	hollyhock
awabi	abalone shell used for iridescent inlays
bakemono	monsters or goblins usually in humanoid form
baku	legendary animal that eats bad dreams
bento-bako	picnic box
bunko	document box
chidori	small birds, usually petrels, shown skimming over water
chinkinbori	incised lines filled with gold (or other) lacquer
eboshi	courtier's hat, usually made of lacquered paper, worn for indication of rank. Also called tate-eboshi
ema	votive picture offered in temples
fubako	letter box
fundame	matte gold lacquer
go	artist name. Also game played on board like checkers
guri	lacquer applied and hardened in alternate colored layers, then deeply incised with V-shaped grooves, usually in a spiral design. Usually red and black lacquers, sometimes with yellow
gyobu	large particles of gold applied individually and irregularly to create effect of mosaic ground. Almost identical to *okibirame*
haku	box
Hannya	devil (usually seen in masks)
heidatsu	see *hyomon*
heijin	rough sprinklings of gold dust into lacquer ground (usually black)
hiramakie	see under *makie*
hirame	irregularly formed flakes of gold or silver metallic filings sprinkled on a partially dried black lacquer ground and polished
hirazogan	flat inlay in metal work
Hogen	honorary art title (sometimes spelled Hogan)
ho-o	phoenix (sometimes spelled ho-ho)
hossu	fly whisk
hyomon	technique in which design is cut out of thin sheets of gold or silver and applied to lacquer
ikakeji	ancient technique of fine gold ground sprinkled with additional large flecks of gold

iroye	colored lacquers
ishime	lacquer simulating a coarse texture, like stone
joge	top and bottom of inro
jubako	tiered food container
kagamibuta	form of netsuke with a metallic disc encased in a shallow round bowl
kakihan	artistic monogram or written personal seal
kamakura-bori	form of carving coated with red and black lacquer
kanagu	clasp on tobacco pouch (omote kanagu—outside metal atachment). Same as kanemono
kanemono	see kanagu
kanoko	"deer" spots in lacquer. Large *hirame* flakes spaced to suggest coat of fawn
kanshitsu	dry lacquer
karako	child
karakusa	arabesques in floral patterns
katakiri	technique of metal engraving using a chisel
kebori	fine hair-line carving
kesobumi-uri	love-letter vendor
kimpun	very fine gold powder
kingi	polished gold lacquer
kirikane or *kirigane*	small inlaid squares or rectangles of gold foil
kiseruzutsu	pipecase, often written tsutsu
	Aikuchi-zutsu. Pipecase of two parts; the insert enters the sheath but is stopped "mouth to mouth"
	Muso-zutso. Pipecase of two parts; the insert enters the sheath without restraint. (Most popular type of zutsu)
	Otoshi-zutsu. Single-piece pipecase with one end open which receives pipe
	Senryu-zutsu. Single-piece pipecase, cut out so that the bowl of the pipe fits into a slit and the mouth of the pipe is enveloped at other end for secure positioning
koban	alloy of three parts silver and one part gold powders
kobako	incense container. Also see kogo
kodogu	incense ceremony set
kogo	small incense container
kore	"this"
kozuka	handle of thin knife accompanying the sword
kuromakie	black design on black ground. Also see *yamamakie* (same thing)
Kyohime	young girl who fell passionately in love with the priest, Anchin, and, turning into a dragon, burned him alive in Dojoji bell
makie	sprinkled picture—general term for the various decorative techniques of sprinkling gold and silver powder onto the lacquered design while the lacquer is still damp

	Hiramakie. Lacquer of slightly raised relief, the design being almost level with the ground
	Takamakie. Lacquer design raised in high relief
manju	"button" netsuke, usually round, either solid or in two sections fitted together
mikuji-bako	divining box to tell fortune
minogame	long-tailed turtle, symbol of long life
mizuire	water dropper. Same as suiteki
mokume	lacquer simulating wood grain
mon	family crests
Moso	one of twenty-four paragons of filial piety, who found bamboo shoots in dead of winter to make soup for ailing mother
namazu	earthquake fish
nanako	"fish roe" surface in metal work, produced by innumerable strokes of a tiny concave punch
nashiji	lacquer ground of gold or silver dust, or very small flakes, buried in transparent lacquer, giving effect of "pearskin," often called aventurine
	E-nashiji: nashiji used for the design rather than for ground
	Mura-nashiji: nashiji used in irregular dense masses, creating a cloud effect
	Yasuriko-nashiji: nashiji using large gold filings, instead of dust, densely applied
negoro	red over black lacquer, polished out to give a blotched effect
nue	legendary beast with monkey head, badger back, dragon scales, and snake tail
nurimono	lacquered objects
nunome	lacquer technique imitating cloth
okibirame	see *gyobu.* Sometimes spelled *okihirame*
oni	small devil
raden	inlaid mother-of-pearl decoration. Also called *aogai*
Raken	chief disciple of Buddha
rogin	brownish-silver lacquer ground
roiro	highly polished black lacquer ground
sabi	lacquer used for high relief design
Saigyo Hoshi	priest who traveled in retirement, usually shown at foot of Mt. Fuji
saku	made, or carved
same-nuri	technique of lacquering sharkskin or rayskin
saya	sheath (inro or sword sheath)
sentoku	alloy in metal, pale yellowish brown in color
shakuhachi	Japanese flute or recorder
shibayama	inlays of mother-of-pearl, ivory, hardstones, etc.
shibuichi	copper-silver alloy, silvery in appearance
shitan-nuri	lacquer imitation of red sandalwood

sho	musical instrument composed of 22 pipes, like pipes of Pan
shukin	gold lacquer covered with red lacquer which is ground down as in *togidashi*. As surface catches light it appears alternately gold or red
somada	see *aogai*, but *somada* is usually greenish shell
sumie	ink painting on lacquer, done with *sumi*, Chinese black ink, usually in *togidashi* technique
suzuribako	writing box
takamakie	see *makie*
takazogan	high inlay in metal work
takarabune	treasure ship of Happy Gods
tebako	lady's cosmetic box
ten-chi	same as joge, i.e. top and bottom of inro: *ten* is top, *chi* is bottom
tengu	legendary winged creature
	Karasu tengu. Has bird body and vicious beak. Often shown climbing out of egg
	Konoha tengu. Long-nosed humanoid who wears tiny hat of the mountain priests
tensho	seal script
to	knife-cut
togidashi	technique in which many coats of lacquer are applied over the finished (sprinkled) design and then polished down with greatest care until the design reappears, resulting in an absolutely even, flat surface. Gives a lovely, shimmering effect
tomobaku	box attesting authenticity of contents, as to artist
tsuba	sword guard
tsugaru	lacquer ground in several colors unevenly applied
tsuikoku	carved black lacquer
tsuishu	carved red lacquer
tsukuru	made
tsuzumi	two-ended drum
uchiwa	fan (not folded fan)
umimatsu	sea pine, a form of black coral
uraza	metal piece "seat" for kanagu or kanemono, *under* pouch flap
urushi	lacquer or lacquerware. Also refers to lacquer tree. *Urushi-e* is lacquer painting
wakaza-nuri	marbled lacquer ground, similar to *tsugaru-nuri*, but with stronger yellow and browns and with gold and silver foil. Pine needles, leaves, etc. sometimes pressed into lower layers of lacquer
yamamakie	black design on black ground. Same as *kuromakie*
zo	made by
zogan-nuri	technique imitating cloisonné; inlays of gold or silver wire are covered with layers of lacquer and rubbed down until the wire reappears

BIBLIOGRAPHY

Ballot, M. J., *Les Laques D'Extrême Orient, Chine et Japon,* ed. G. Vanest, Paris et Bruxelles, 1927

Boyer, Martha, *Catalogue of Japanese Lacquers in the Walters Art Gallery,* Baltimore, Maryland, 1970

*Bushell, R., *The Inro Handbook,* Weatherhill, Tokyo, 1979

Casal, U. A., "Inro," *Transactions and Proceedings of the Japan Society of London,* Vol. XXXVII, London, 1941

*Casal, U. A., *Japanese Art Lacquers,* Monumenta Nipponica Monograph No. 18, Sophia University, Tokyo, 1961

Casal, U. A., *Catalogue of Inro in the U. A. Casal Collection,* Osaka City Museum, Kyoto, 1973, T. Sakai ed. (in Japanese)

Catalogue of Japanese Lacquer, 2 vols., ed. by E. F. Strange, Victoria and Albert Museum, London, 1925

Catalogue of the M. T. Hindson Collection of Important Japanese Works of Art, Sotheby & Co., London, 20 October 1968 (auction catalogue)

Catalogue of the Seymour Trower Collection, ed. by Henri L. Joly, Glendining and Company, London 1913

Catalogue of the W. L. Behrens Collection, ed. by Henri L. Joly, Glendining and Company, London, 1913–14

Davey, Neil K., *Netsuke,* Sotheby Parke Bernet Publications Ltd., New York, 1974

Dean, M., *Japanese Lacquer—An Exposition,* Tokyo, 1984

Ducros, A., *Netsuke and Sagemono,* Paris, 1987

Eskenazi Ltd., *Japanese Lacquer from the Verbrugge Collection,* London, 1989

*Eskenazi Ltd., *Charles A. Greenfield Collection of Japanese Lacquer,* London, 1990

Getty Conservation Institute, *Urushi,* Tokyo, 1988

Gonse, L., *L'Art Japonais,* Paris, 1883

Hana no Masegaki (catalogue in Japanese) ed. Morimasa Takei, 8 vols., Tokyo, 1917 (no publisher indicated)

Hart, Ernest, "Notes on the History of Lacquer," *Transactions and Proceedings of the Japan Society of London,* Vol. III, December 22, 1893

Herberts, K., *Oriental Lacquer, Art and Technique,* Henry N. Abrams, Inc., New York, 1963

*Jahss, Melvin and Betty, *Inro and Other Miniature Forms of Japanese Lacquer Art,* Charles E. Tuttle Company, Rutland, Vermont and Tokyo, Japan, 1971

Joli, Henry L. and Kumasaku Tomita, *Japanese Art and Handicraft,* Yamanaka & Company, London, 1916 (known as the Red Cross Catalogue)

Jonas, F. M., *Netsuke,* Kegan Paul, Trench, Trubner & Company, London, 1928 (contains a list of lacquerers)

Klefisch-Kumaro, *The Champoud Collection,* Kyoto, 1984

Koizumi, G., *Lacquer Work,* Sir Isaac Pitman & Sons, Ltd., London 1925

Link, H. *The Art of Shibata Zeshin,* Honolulu, 1979

Morse, Edward S., *Japanese Homes and Their Surroundings,* Ticknor & Company, Boston, 1886

Okada, B., *A Sprinkling of Gold,* New Jersey, 1983

Orange, James, *Japanese Lacquers,* Kelly & Walsh, Ltd., Yokohama, 1910

Pekarik, A. J., *Japanese Lacquer, 1600–1900,* Metropolitan Museum, N.Y., 1980

Rasmussen, Jens and E. A. Wrangham, "Inro," *Arts of Asia,* Vol. 7, No. 3, May–June 1977

Reikichi, Ueda, as adapted by Raymond Bushell, *The Netsuke Handbook,* Charles E. Tuttle Company, Rutland, Vermont, and Tokyo, Japan, 1961

Reinaecher, Victor, "Japanese Lacquer," *Transactions and Proceedings of the Japan Society of London,* Vol. XXXVI, London, 1939

―――, "Masterpieces of Japanese Craftmanship," *Country Life Annual,* 1955, pp. 52ff.

Roberts, Laurance, P., *A Dictionary of Japanese Artists,* Weatherhill, Tokyo and New York, 1976

*Scheenberger, P. F., *The Baur Collection of Japanese Lacquer,* Geneva, 1984

Stern, Harold P., *The Magnificent Three: Lacquer, Netsuke and Tsuba* (Selections from the Collection of Charles A. Greenfield), Japan Society, Inc., New York, 1972

*Takayama Inro Museum, *Inro and Netsuke—Epitome of Edo Culture,* Takayama, 1990

Tomkinson, Michael, *A Japanese Collection,* 2 vols., George Allen, London, 1898

Von Rague, Beatrix, *A History of Japanese Lacquerwork,* University of Toronto Press, Toronto and Buffalo, 1976

Weber, V. F., *Koji Hoten,* 2 vols., privately printed, Paris, 1926 (in French)

Wrangham, E. A., *Catalogue of an Exhibition of Japanese Inro,* E. A. Wrangham and the Ashmolean Museum, Oxford, 1973

Yonemura, Ann, *Japanese Lacquer, Freer Gallery,* Washington D. C., 1979

Yoshino, Tomio, *Japanese Lacquer Ware,* Japan Travel Bureau, Tokyo, 1959

*most useful for beginners

ACKNOWLEDGMENTS

We gratefully acknowledge the generous support for this publication by the following individuals and companies:

Nordskog Industries
Mr. and Mrs. Dennis Stanfill
Mrs. Emma Dagan
Toyota Motors Inc., U.S.A.
Several anonymous donors

―――――――

Pacific Asia Museum has been substantially funded by a generous grant from the W. M. Keck Foundation.